POLITICS OF DEFEAT

POLITICS OF DEFEAT

THE DECLINE OF THE
LIBERAL PARTY IN SASKATCHEWAN

BARRY WILSON

Western Producer Prairie Books
Saskatoon, Saskatchewan

Cover design by John Luckhurst
Printed and bound in Canada by MODERN PRESS

Saskatoon, Saskatchewan

Western Producer Prairie Books publications are
produced and manufactured in the middle of
western Canada by a unique publishing venture
owned by a group of prairie farmers who are
members of Saskatchewan Wheat Pool. Our first
book in 1954 was a reprint of a serial originally
carried in *The Western Producer*, a weekly
newspaper serving western Canadian farmers
since 1923. We continue the tradition of
providing enjoyable and informative reading for
all Canadians.

Canadian Cataloguing in Publication Data

Wilson, Barry, 1948-
    Politics of defeat

    Includes index.
    ISBN 0-88833-058-8

  1. Saskatchewan Liberal Association.
  2. Liberal Party (Canada). Saskatchewan.
  3. Saskatchewan — Politics and government.
  I. Title.
  JL319.A54W54   324.27124'06   C80-091043-5

To Sarah and Cynthia, who are the future;
and to Verne, a good friend when it mattered.

CONTENTS

PREFACE

INTRODUCTION   1

Chapter One
THE POLITICS OF VICTORY   7

Chapter Two
THE YEARS IN POWER   13

Chapter Three
THE STEUART YEARS BEGIN   23

Chapter Four
A PARTY MAN AS LEADER   33

Chapter Five
AN ATTEMPT AT REORGANIZATION   43

Chapter Six
FINANCES AND FEDERAL LIBERALS   51

Chapter Seven
IN SEARCH OF A POLICY   59

Chapter Eight
THE POLITICAL WARS, 1972-75   71

Chapter Nine
THE 1975 RACE FOR POWER   87

Chapter Ten
A PARTY DIVIDED   99

Chapter Eleven
IN SEARCH OF A LEADER   111

Chapter Twelve
THE MALONE YEARS   121

Chapter Thirteen
THE CAMPAIGN DISASTER, 1978   139

Chapter Fourteen
DEFEAT OF THE LANG GANG   155

Epilogue
AFTERMATH OF DEFEAT   159

INDEX   167

PREFACE

The recent history of the Liberal party in Saskatchewan is more than the story of the rise and fall of a provincial or regional political organization. It is the story, complex and often dramatic, of how the Liberal party lost its last significant western Canadian foothold.

The policies of the Liberal party encouraged the opening of the Prairies at the turn of the century and provincial Liberal politicians were the primary spokesmen for the region in the early decades of the twentieth century. Gradually, that power declined. Alberta voters started the trend in 1921 when they threw out an entrenched Liberal regime to elect a then-radical United Farmers of Alberta government. Fourteen years later, the UFA was replaced by the Social Credit party and the Liberal decline continued. It has not elected an MLA since 1967. In Manitoba, the Liberal-Progressive party was voted out of power in 1958 after more than two decades of consecutive victories. During the next twenty years, Liberals were reduced to a fringe party as the Conservatives and New Democratic Party alternated in power. In 1979, the sole remaining Liberal MLA resigned his seat to run federally.

Throughout this period, Saskatchewan was different. The Liberal party remained either the government or the only viable alternative long after it had ceased to be a significant force in the sister prairie provinces.

The seventies changed that. During the last two years of the decade, Liberals fell from grace in the province, both provincially and federally. The eighties dawned without a single Liberal elected to provincial or federal office from Saskatchewan for the first time in the province's history. The last prairie outpost had been lost.

This book tells the story of that decline. It is an outsider's view, part history and part journalism.

The author drew material from a number of sources: personal experience during six years as a Saskatchewan journalist, reporting on and watching the Liberal party; scores of interviews with Liberal politicians and workers, political opponents, friends and foes; and extensive reading of the public record as it chronicled the highs and lows of the party and its personalities.

Many of the people interviewed cooperated only if they remained anonymous. That commitment has been honored in the text. Others kindly agreed to totally on-the-record interviews. In all cases, their recollections and assessments were valuable.

In particular, the author would like to thank Saskatchewan Liberal leader Ted Malone and former leader Senator Dave Steuart for this cooperation. They both granted several long interviews, answered all questions put to them and tolerated persistent intrusions into their public and personal lives.

To all who cooperated in the research, writing, and criticism which made this text possible, I offer my thanks. Any errors of fact or perception are the sole responsibility of the author.

INTRODUCTION

In the federal election of May 22, 1979, the Liberal party virtually disappeared in Saskatchewan after more than seven decades of influence, relevance, and often power. During the previous two decades, the province had been the last dependable refuge the party had on the Prairies.

The final humiliation came at the hands of federal voters who defeated every Liberal candidate in the province's fourteen ridings, including three members of the previous Parliament. Every Liberal ran third, including the powerful minister of transport, Otto Lang, in Saskatoon East. The party's share of the popular vote fell below 22 percent from more than 30 percent in 1974. With no elected members and no obvious leader, the party was in a shambles.

Nine months later, in the federal election of February 18, 1980, voters reaffirmed their decision. No Liberals were elected, despite strenuous party campaign efforts to convince Saskatchewan voters they should be represented in a majority Liberal government.

The federal defeat was really just a postscript, however. The fatal blow to the party came seven months earlier when Saskatchewan Liberals gathered at the Hotel Saskatchewan in Regina to watch in stunned silence as their party was wiped off the political map. In the provincial election of October 18, 1978, not a single Liberal was elected to the Legislature for the first time in the seventy-three-year history of the province. The party lost the eleven seats it had carried into the election, gathering less than 14 percent of the popular vote. It ended an era, possibly a lifetime, for Saskatchewan's oldest political party.

What had happened? Why did the federal party return to its 1960s impotence after eleven years of resurgence under Otto Lang's guidance? And why had a provincial party which had ruled the province as recently as 1971 virtually disappeared?

For the federal wing, the answers lay partly in the national disenchantment which threw the national Liberal government out of power after sixteen unbroken years. Organizational flaws, local personalities, and the lack of a provincial base were also to blame.

For the provincial wing, the answers are more complex. In part, it was the failure of the twenty-eight-day campaign which preceded that devastating October night and the errors of the previous two years under new leader Ted Malone. At least part of the answer also lies in the history of this unusual prairie political organization.

The Liberal party of Saskatchewan has always been a difficult entity to define and describe. By most measures, it is a Canadian political success story. It is one of western Canada's most durable electoral machines, tracing its roots to the years immediately preceding Saskatchewan's 1905 creation as a province.

While Liberal parties in Manitoba, Alberta, and British Columbia disappeared or headed in that direction, the Saskatchewan Liberals maintained a viable organization. During the province's first seventy-three years, the party held power for forty years. It formed the first provincial administration under Sir Walter Scott, and succeeding leaders W. M. Martin, C. A. Dunning and Jimmy Gardiner maintained the tradition for twenty-four unbroken years. It was the era when the province was opened, and through a combination of patronage and consensus policies, the party forged a coalition of rural and immigrant interests which made its power base in those years almost unassailable.[1]

In 1929, the tide turned and J. T. M. Anderson swept to power on the strength of a coalition between his Conservatives and a strange collection of groups, ranging from the Progressives to the Ku Klux Klan. But his government was unable to cope effectively with the devastation of the Depression years, and in 1934 Gardiner led the Liberals back into power. A year later, William Patterson became the fifth Liberal premier when Gardiner followed many of his predecessors to Ottawa and a place in the federal government — in his case, the agriculture portfolio and responsibility for federal Liberal fortunes in Saskatchewan.

At first, Patterson seemed destined to continue the Liberal dominance of provincial politics. In the 1938 election, Liberals won fifty of fifty-five seats and the party seemed secure. But the magic was wearing off as the Co-operative Commonwealth Federation, social democratic child of the Depression, began to score some organizational triumphs around the province. Through defections and by-election losses, Liberal Legislature strength had dropped to thirty-three when Patterson called the election for summer 1944. The election results confirmed the Liberal decline and created a stir around the world — five Liberals were elected to face

---

[1] An excellent history of the Liberal party, its policies and impact on the developing Saskatchewan can be found in *Prairie Liberalism* (Toronto: University of Toronto Press, 1975), by University of Saskatchewan professor David Smith.

forty-seven CCF members under North America's first democratic socialist premier, Baptist preacher T. C. Douglas.

The election shock began a long Liberal term in the wilderness, plagued by unappealing policies and weak provincial leadership. In fact, part of the leadership problem lay with the powerful influence of the federal Liberal party then in power in Ottawa. When Gardiner joined the government of Prime Minister William Lyon Mackenzie King, he took effective control of the provincial party with him. Patterson had been a protege, and Gardiner was able to influence and direct him. Federal dominance continued after a 1946 leadership shuffle which put lawyer Walter Tucker into the leader's office and later through the brief tenure of Opposition House Leader Asmundur Loptson, who replaced Tucker on an interim basis in 1953 when the provincial leader unsuccessfully tried to join Gardiner in Ottawa.

By then, the federal influence was increasingly being seen as a problem by provincial Liberals. The CCF exploited the link to heap scorn on provincial Liberals for unpopular federal Liberal programs. Delegates to the 1954 provincial leadership convention tried to rectify that by electing A. H. (Hammy) McDonald as leader. He was a Legislature veteran who was not viewed as a Gardiner surrogate, and delegates hoped he would be able to break the federal Liberal hold on the party. It was a false hope, and when McDonald's leadership failed to catch on, the shadow of Jimmy Gardiner returned to take control. In fact, it took Saskatchewan Tory John Diefenbaker to end the Gardiner influence. In the 1958 Diefenbaker sweep of the country, Gardiner lost his Melville riding after forty-three consecutive years as either an MLA or MP.

At first, it appeared this new-found freedom might have come too late for the provincial party. The absence of control from Ottawa was matched by a vacuum of leadership, policy, and fighting will in the provincial party. It was clearly time for a change.

Enter Moose Jaw merchant Ross Thatcher and Prince Albert merchant Dave Steuart, the nucleus of a new Liberal team which within five years had rebuilt the party organization, revitalized and inspired opponents of the CCF, and defeated the twenty-year-old government. For the next seven years, the party ruled Saskatchewan. The circle had been completed.

Yet despite this not insignificant success, the party has often appeared to be a candidate for demise. In 1956 when the Liberals had been twelve years out of office, Premier Douglas predicted they were a "spent force in Saskatchewan politics." Eight years later, Thatcher proved him wrong. In 1973, out of power again, leader Steuart told a party convention in Calgary that Liberalism could die throughout the West if Liberals did not work harder. "We haven't fought hard enough for the West," he said.

The problem which Steuart and others have seen is that the party always had to walk a tightrope between representing western provincial interests and being aligned with the federal Liberal party, which is seen in the West as a party dominated by the protectionist, big business interests of Ontario and Quebec. Since 1944, the provincial party has been most successful when it keeps the federal party at arm's length or treats it as an enemy. But the attraction and power of the oft-ruling federal party are often hard to resist or repulse.

The other major problem for Saskatchewan Liberals is that they have never been able consistently to fit into the class politics which have evolved in the province since the left-wing populist Co-operative Commonwealth Federation and its New Democratic Party successor came onto the scene in the 1930s. The CCF built a coalition of left, farm, and labor voters which it was able to hold together for twenty years. It was a class response to the hardship and inequities of the Depression years when the image of chartered banks and free enterprise took a beating on the Prairies. The Liberals had been accustomed to governing through broad consensus and they found it difficult to formulate policies which would either challenge the dominance of the CCF over working class voters and portions of the middle class or effectively mobilize the rest of the population under one banner. In the absence of effective policies, the party often fell back on almost meaningless antisocialist rhetoric which usually failed to excite.

By the early 1960s, the CCF government had been twenty years in power. For many, it had become entrenched and too far removed from its original principles. New Liberal leader Ross Thatcher was able to capitalize on these feelings of discontent and to mobilize voters against the CCF with promises of efficient government and prosperity.

Portions of the NDP-CCF coalition held together but Thatcher's genius was in being able to stake out those parts of the population not clearly in the NDP camp. It was a form of class politics and it worked. In the process, the Liberal government made little attempt to attract organized labor, intellectuals, or other groups it felt were "the enemy." The Liberals won power in two consecutive elections.

Then, after seven years of government, the Liberal coalition fell apart under the strain of a faltering economy, policies too rigid for the changing public mood, and Thatcher's abrasive style of politics. The task facing the party after its 1971 defeat was to learn from the mistakes and accomplishments of the previous seven years and start again. Thatcher had proved it could be done.

This book examines the party's attempts to come back and its dramatic failure. Through a series of leaders, policies, and tactics, it struggled to remain a viable force. But the party was still burdened with the blind spots of the past as well as a new challenge — a third party threat from the right wing that Liberals had always assumed was their territory without asking.

The book also details the collapse of the federal vote in 1979. However, with the cyclical history of federal Liberal support in the province and the effect of federal Liberal fortunes on the provincial wing, the failure to elect an MP could well have been just a temporary setback. It has happened before and, with a solid base on which to build, federal Liberal fortunes in Saskatchewan could rebound with a national upswing in Liberal favor.

The decimation of the provincial party was a more significant and potentially more final verdict.

The book is a study of Liberal politics in the contemporary prairie culture, the struggle for life by a political organization many insisted on consigning to the museum of ideas whose day had passed. From fund-raising techniques to leadership convention intrigues, it is the story of a political organization in the throes of change and under the strain of challenge.

In the end, it is a profile of a failure so complete the organization may never be able to rebound. After October 18, 1978, many were predicting the Saskatchewan Liberal party had been permanently relegated to the history books. If the prediction proves correct, the political complexion of western Canada's most politically lively province will have been profoundly and permanently changed.

Chapter One

THE POLITICS OF VICTORY

It was, by all accounts, an extraordinary meeting at the King's Hotel in Regina on a July day in 1959 when the Saskatchewan Liberal party deposed its leader. It was a day of high political drama in a political party without a tradition of turning on its leaders. It marked a turning point in the history of the party — the beginning of a rebuilding which would put it into power in the province in less than five years.

The victim that day was A. H. (Hammy) McDonald, an eleven-year veteran of the Legislature with five years as party leader. They had not been good years for the party, which had been in Opposition since 1944. Although he started a reorganization and tried to involve the membership in policy making, McDonald had been unable to make major gains against the governing CCF. In 1956, he had increased Legislature representation to fourteen seats from ten, but he had also watched the Social Credit party win three seats and 21.5 percent of the popular vote — just 9 percent less than the Liberals. There were worries in some quarters that the party could lose the Official Opposition status to the Socreds. Others worried about the Progressive Conservative sweeps of Saskatchewan by former provincial PC leader John Diefenbaker in the 1957 and 1958 federal elections. To make matters worse, McDonald reported to the executive in June that the Liberal party was broke and memberships were down. He had argued that with a provincial election likely within a year, the best tactic might be for the party to lie low, try to consolidate, and not expend too much energy fighting what would be a losing battle. He had shown what he meant by not campaigning as hard as some party officials felt he should in the June 3 Kinistino by-election, which the CCF won. McDonald was away for part of the campaign.

Some segments of the party, now used to being in Opposition and still reeling from the federal Liberal defeats in the 1957 and 1958 elections, appeared willing to accept that proposed strategy. But for a group on the provincial executive, led by Prince Albert merchant and civic politician Dave Steuart, it was time to challenge what they saw as growing defeatism.

The plan for a leadership challenge was developed during a night of talking and drinking among a handful of executive members and key party personnel in early July. They felt comfortable suggesting a leadership change because, for the first time in years, they had an alternative — Moose Jaw merchant Ross Thatcher, a former CCF MP who had left the party, joined the federal Liberal party, and spent the past three years offering attention-grabbing criticism of the CCF. The next morning, the group drove to Moose Jaw to talk to Thatcher. He told them he would not talk about the leadership until a convention had been called and McDonald was no longer leader.

Steuart took the hint. He quickly drove to McDonald's home at Moosomin in southeast Saskatchewan to confront the leader. McDonald angrily refused Steuart's proposal to resign and the meeting ended bitterly. Until then, the rumblings had been confined to Liberal circles but word of Steuart's confrontation with McDonald appeared in the weekly *Yorkton Enterprise* and as the story spread, along with recriminations over who might have leaked it, a major crisis of leadership quickly developed within the party.

It came to a head at an executive meeting in Regina. As the meeting started, Steuart took to the attack, arguing the party had to become more aggressive and proposing that if McDonald did not want to lead that move, there might be a candidate in the wings who would. McDonald defended himself and appealed for loyalty. The executive appeared split, but there was obviously some support for Steuart's argument. It was, Steuart said later, "quite an emotional scene." It ended when McDonald left the meeting to consider his options in the face of opposition.

He soon sent a message announcing his resignation (although he continued to be a key Liberal MLA until a 1965 appointment to the Senate, where he stayed until his death in 1980). The stage was set for a leadership convention to try to find someone to restore the party to the glories it had once known.

To the Steuart group in the party in 1959, that meant Ross Thatcher. They found his brand of antisocialism exciting because he spoke with the authority of one who had been there. He attacked the CCF on grounds of mismanagement, but he also charged the moderates in the party were being shoved aside by the "dogmatic socialists" who would have the state run everything. To fight the threat, Thatcher argued, a free-enterprise party should offer the alternative of an improved business climate and greatly increased capital investment to create prosperity and better times. It would require a well-disciplined, aggressive political organization with a will to win and a positive philosophy of small government and efficiency to offer the voters.

To Dave Steuart and his fellow malcontents in the party, this approach was the answer. Steuart had first seen Thatcher speak on behalf of federal Liberal policies at a public park two years earlier and he had been impressed. Now, he was more convinced than ever that Thatcher was the man to pull the Liberals out of their slump. "He had lots of energy and I thought he made sense," Steuart says.

But would Thatcher agree to run? At forty-two years of age, he had already been an MP for twelve years, had been defeated in two attempts (1957 and 1958) to win election as a federal Liberal MP, and had turned down an offer to lead the provincial Social Credit party. After efforts began to organize a Thatcher campaign committee in the wake of McDonald's decision to resign, Steuart went back to see Thatcher, to ask that he let his name stand in the scheduled September leadership vote.

Thatcher struck a hard bargain. He said he would run if conditions were met — he wanted money in the bank to finance an organizing drive and he wanted commitments from a number of prominent Liberals that they would run in the next election. Steuart also had to agree to run for president at the convention so he could help lead the revitalization. The conditions were met and, despite opposition from caucus members and three other candidates, Thatcher was elected the ninth leader of the provincial Leader party on the first ballot at the convention. Steuart was elected president.

The man chosen to lead the Liberals out of the doldrums was a complex, powerful figure. He operated a prosperous Moose Jaw retail business and his views were strongly in favor of business and development, against powerful government. Yet he had been elected to Parliament in 1945 on the first serious wave of CCF popularity, sitting for the next ten years as a member of a party which preached the benefits of the welfare state and more powerful government. Thatcher was an able politician, a good organizer, and a powerful personality who could attract both devoted followers and rabid opponents. He was ambitious, hard-working, and demanding of others. Above all, he was uncompromising in his principles, totally convinced his vision of the world was the correct one to which events and people would conform.

His actions showed him to be a courageous man, prepared to take risks for his ideas. When he became disillusioned with the CCF and increasingly isolated in caucus, he rose in Parliament in 1952 to denounce a Liberal government proposal to introduce old age pensions. The CCF strongly supported the Liberal government on this issue. It was an unpopular speech within the party and won him the wrath both of his caucus colleagues and of supporters back home. Thatcher would not back down from his views and left the party within two years, joining the Liberals after a brief stint as an independent MP. In 1956, he burned his final CCF bridges with a Commons speech denouncing the record of the CCF government in Saskatchewan and its use of Crown corporations. When he decided in 1957 to run for the Liberals against former CCF colleague Hazen Argue in Assiniboia riding of southern Saskatchewan, he found himself battling

Premier Douglas as well. His attack on Crown corporations became a major issue, and a public debate between Thatcher and Douglas in Mossbank, Saskatchewan, in May 1957 was broadcast by radio across the province. Thatcher was rapidly gaining credibility as the most articulate opponent of the CCF, but when the ballots were counted in Assiniboia, he had lost. He returned to Moose Jaw with an uncertain political future but a growing reputation as a politician not afraid to fight for his beliefs. The high profile helped dispel the suspicion and fallout which usually plague a turncoat politician. After he left the CCF caucus in Parliament, *The Calgary Herald* said of Thatcher: "Colorful and well-liked as he was, Mr. Thatcher just never looked right sitting in the CCF ranks anyway. He was an anachronism, a wealthy young capitalist merchant sitting among lean, hungry and non-capitalist socialists."

But would all this be enough? Given the low state of party popularity and morale, the task ahead was enormous. Thatcher quickly put his energy and ambition to work travelling the province, rounding up candidates, raising money, selling memberships, and spelling out his vision of the Saskatchewan future. Steuart was his backup man, often accompanying the leader on his tours. The party they inherited was badly disorganized, far removed from the fighting trim Thatcher wanted to see. "Since the thirties, the party had become fat, unwilling to do the groundwork necessary to win elections," Steuart says. "They were always looking for a gimmick. But there is only one gimmick in politics and that is to go across the streets into the kitchens and motivate people."

By November, seven organizers were in the field and the party deficit had been replaced by a small surplus, in part because of the introduction of paid memberships.

In 1960 came the next election, and although Thatcher's drive for office fell far short, the party did make gains while the Social Credit party popularity declined. (The Progressive Conservatives under new leader Martin Pederson also made some gains.) Final results were: CCF, thirty-eight, for a gain of two; Liberals, seventeen, for a gain of three. The Social Credit Party was reduced to 12 percent of the popular vote and no seats. The PCs climbed to 14 percent of the vote but also won no seats. It was a moral victory and a psychological boost for the Liberals, master-minded by Thatcher's organizing efforts, his strong drive to win, and a policy platform based on 1959 convention resolutions which included both expanded social programs and a major new emphasis on private develop-ment to pay the bills.

The years after the 1960 election were exciting ones for Saskatchewan Liberals. After sixteen years in Opposition, they had hope. Thatcher and Steuart continued their organizing travels, and both funds and member-ships soared. Soon, political events and the all-important electoral scoreboard began to work in favor of the Liberals as well. The most important issue of that era was the decision by the CCF to establish a prepaid universal system of medical care in the province. In the months before the 1960 election, both Liberals and CCF had supported such a scheme, and at first it seemed widely popular. But after the election, relations between the Douglas administration and the province's doctors began to sour. Doctors began to argue the CCF proposals would infringe on their professional freedom, with the spectre of "socialized medicine" always in the background. The government decided to push the scheme through, and legislation was approved establishing medicare and bringing it into force July 1, 1962, under the supervision of a Medical Care Insurance Commission. The doctors argued the CCF had broken an earlier promise to implement medicare only with the approval of the medical profession, and when marathon talks failed to bring a settlement by July 1, most doctors in the province closed their doors. It was the first doctors' strike in North America and it lasted for twenty-three days until a mediator worked out an agreement during meetings in Saskatoon.

While claiming support for the principle of prepaid medical care insurance, the Liberals were able to score significant points during the medicare crisis. With the threat of a doctors' strike, Keep Our Doctors (KOD) committees formed in communities around the province. They were the centre of local opposition to the CCF, and many Liberals played key roles in these KOD committees. In Prince Albert, for example, Dave Steuart was one of the leaders of a very vocal committee, and the Liberal party became the provincial voice for the committees' arguments. Liberals fought the legislation in the House and charged the government with dictatorial methods and with threatening the health care needs of the province in the interests of its socialistic schemes. During the height of the storm, Liberals picked up support by opposing medicare. However, they also knew when to change tactics. By 1964, the program was working and party officials felt it was winning approval. Then the Liberal emphasis changed to making medicare work better, rather than getting rid of it.

The medicare fight was just one side of the growing Liberal momentum. It also started to show in by-election victories. On February 22, 1961, a Liberal won the Turtleford by-election called after the courts overturned the narrow victory of a CCF candidate in the 1960 general election. In 1961, in the midst of the medicare fight, the CCF leader and premier, T. C. Douglas, left the province to take on the federal leadership of the newly-formed New Democratic Party. A Liberal won the Weyburn seat Douglas had held since 1944. Eleven months later, in November 1962, the Liberals made it three in a row when Steuart swept to power in a Prince Albert by-election. His victory margin was 2,522 votes in the traditionally CCF seat.

The by-election victories were important indicators that the Liberal electoral machine was beginning to work again. But the 1962 defection to the Liberals of J. Walter Erb was an equally important boost. It showed the CCF machine was in trouble.

Erb was a longtime CCF member who had been health minister when the medicare issue surfaced. He had played a key role in getting the legislation drawn up and the negotiations with doctors underway. But when he began to have doubts as doctor opposition increased, he was removed from the health portfolio and put in charge of public works. Erb was not happy and he chose carefully the time to let it be known. On May 3, as Premier Woodrow Lloyd prepared to address a specially-called meeting of doctors in Regina, the *Regina Leader-Post* appeared, announcing Erb had defected to the Liberals. He accused the CCF of disregarding "political integrity" by moving on medicare without physician approval, and in the days that followed, he charged that the government had been less than honest in its dealings on medicare and that the CCF had become a tool for organized labor.

It was music to Liberal ears. Erb's charges coincided with themes Thatcher was trying to emphasize as he crisscrossed the province looking for votes. With an organizational effort centred around constituency meetings, an impressive series of victories building up, and attractive candidates jumping aboard the bandwagon, a Liberal victory in 1964 seemed conceivable. The CCF, feeling the loss of Douglas and still reeling from the backlash against the way the medicare issue had been handled, was simply hanging on.

The election came in April 1964, and Liberals campaigned primarily on the argument that the CCF had brought economic stagnation to the province but it could be reversed if Liberals were elected to improve the business climate. There were also promises of advances in social programs, better treatment for the province's native population, and more efficient government. The main message, however, was economic — if voters wanted to savor the good life and economic prosperity, elect the Liberals and investment would follow.

Election night confirmed the Liberal optimism. Liberals elected thirty-two; NDP elected twenty-six; PCs elected one. The Liberals won a fraction more of the popular vote than the NDP — 40.31 percent versus 40.21 percent — while the PCs under Pederson climbed to their best showing in decades with 19 percent. But it was a Liberal victory and a Liberal night. Ross Thatcher had returned the party to power.

Chapter Two

THE YEARS IN POWER

The new premier established his style of leadership within days: it would be an austere, hard-working government, and Ross Thatcher would be very much in control. The morning after the election, some aides were astounded when they received early-morning calls from Thatcher to get them into the office, even though many had been celebrating late into the night. More indicative was Thatcher's approach to his cabinet ministers on the day they were sworn in. Several members of the 1964 caucus, including Steuart, say that on the day of the swearing-in ceremony, Thatcher asked the new ministers to sign an undated letter of resignation which he could use whenever he felt the need. Steuart says when there was strong resistance to the idea, the premier satisfied himself with having them sign pledges that they would try to reduce the size of the civil service in their departments.

He also showed his stubborn side in dealings with the federal Liberal party. Thatcher felt uncomfortable with the federal Liberals, and during his tenure as leader, his skirmishes with the federal wing of his own party were almost as well known as his battles with the "socialists." In part, it was a fight over who would control the party in Saskatchewan. In the wake of the Gardiner era, this was a sensitive issue, and from the beginning Thatcher was determined to be in charge of all aspects of the party on his own turf, both federal and provincial. The first battle was waged at the 1960 annual convention when he clashed with University of Saskatchewan law professor Otto Lang, a Liberal with primarily federalist leanings, over what power the federal wing should be given in the party constitution. Thatcher won his point, that the provincial wing should be supreme, and during the next two years, relations between federal and provincial wings deteriorated to the point where federal leader Lester Pearson appointed Lang to run the 1962 and 1963 federal Saskatchewan campaigns. Thatcher was infuriated, and after he won the premiership, he reclaimed control over federal party affairs in the province. He lost it again to Lang after 1968, and the stalemate continued into the seventies.

A side issue in the battle was a personality clash between Thatcher and his various federal Liberal opponents, ranging from Lang to Pearson and later Pierre Elliot Trudeau. But a large part of it was also disagreement over political tactics and how to deal with the Progressive Conservatives. In Saskatchewan, Thatcher considered the CCF the major opponent, and to dislodge it, he was willing to try to make a deal with the PC party. He openly sought the support of Conservative voters and occasionally courted PC leaders to help him in the fight against the "common enemy." In Ottawa, this was considered heresy. The PCs were the enemy and the CCF was at worst a minor force and at best a potential ally against the powerful Diefenbaker government. The dispute over tactics made the federal party reluctant to play an active role in provincial campaigns which involved attempts at collusion with the PCs. This reluctance was resented by Thatcher and became a major point of disagreement.

Despite the inner-party feuds and Thatcher's growing tendency to one-man rule, the tone of the first term of Liberal government was optimistic. The economy was on the upswing; the open-arm approach to foreign capital brought investment to the potash industry, announcement of a long-sought pulp mill in Prince Albert, and favorable reviews of the provincial "business climate" by outside financiers. With civil service numbers and budgets being restrained and implementation of such symbolic gestures as a cutback in ministerial travel and entertaining, the government appeared to be living up to its promise of frugality.

There were also some advances in social programs. The government made the native population a priority, and through job training and quotas for the civil service and for companies doing business with the government, it hoped to give natives a slice of the economic prosperity Thatcher felt he was helping create. Despite the fears of some and the predictions of the CCF-NDP, medicare and hospitalization systems were retained and the social program advances of the previous government did not suddenly disappear.

In fact, one of the first priorities of the Thatcher government had been to settle the controversy which lingered from the introduction of medicare. In 1964 when the Liberals assumed office, the province was still suffering aftershocks from the 'medicare crisis' and the doctors' strike of 1962. Two years later, communities were still divided and the health care system was being disrupted. It was a delicate issue for the Liberals. They had vigorously fought medicare in Opposition and more than readily cashed in on the anti-CCF passions the issue aroused. It was widely believed the medicare campaign was one of the key factors in the Liberal victory.

However, Liberal party strategists were also quickly concluding that medicare was becoming popular with Saskatchewan voters and any moves to dismantle the program would be risky. Although voters were not entirely happy with the way it had been introduced, they had begun to tire of doctor rhetoric and threats. By 1964, the benefits of the system were becoming obvious.

With strong dissent from some antimedicare Liberals, the government and Health Minister Dave Steuart quickly decided to maintain the system, but to try to make it more efficient.

However, that left Steuart with a major problem — the medicare battle was still being fought in many small hospitals where elected boards were refusing to accredit doctors who had come to Saskatchewan as strike breakers during the crisis. The conservative hospital boards considered them outsiders and CCF supporters.

Before it was defeated, the CCF had tried to cope by amending the Hospital Standards Act to allow the government to accredit doctors over the heads of local hospital boards. The move made the boards dig in, and it became another flashpoint in the perceived battle over local control of health care.

The Liberal dilemma was clear. Much of their rural support came from the type of people who would support the hospital board stand, yet health department officials saw the battle was hurting the quality of health care in rural areas.

Steuart's reluctant solution was to get tough at the risk of alienating his party's natural constituency. He contacted local hospital officials and told them if they did not begin to accredit doctors willing to work in their areas, the hospital would be closed down. Steuart considered it a victory when the hospitals decided he was serious and a form of truce was called in the countryside. Willing doctors were to be accredited.

The immediate crisis was over and for the next two and a half years, Steuart presided over a relatively quiet time for the huge health department. It was a period of consolidation in health programs and, in some ways, a perfect reflection of the differences in attitude between the Thatcher government and its predecessor. The Saskatchewan CCF and NDP considered the health department a key area in their plans for a more humane society and a source of program initiatives to put all citizens on an equal footing, at least for health care purposes. The Liberals viewed the health care system devised by the bureaucrats with suspicion. Health care initiatives were an area they conceded to the NDP. The Steuart years in the health portfolio were largely a time to try to control costs, to keep rein on the bureaucratic social planners with their dreams of more programs. It was also a time to watch reluctantly over the flourishing of the increasingly-accepted medicare system which was a thorn in the side of many free enterprise Liberals.

The same mood existed in other areas of government activity as well. It was not an activist or expanding government. The Liberals moved out of some operations started by the CCF, and there were even discussions with private insurance companies about selling the Saskatchewan Government Insurance Office to the private sector. In the end, potential buyers killed the idea by deciding it would be too expensive.

The government did show itself quick to move in some situations, though. When Thatcher's dream of a better world through business investment and industrialization appeared to be threatened, initiatives were not long in appearing. The government made concessions to attract potash and pulp mill investment, and when labor stoppages appeared to threaten the good life in 1966, legislation was quickly passed to force workers in "essential services" back to work. Saskatchewan Power Corporation employees were the first target.

Thatcher and senior party officials felt this passive yet tough style of government was in line with the public mood, and when the premier called an unexpectedly-early election for October 11, 1967, they were confident of a massive victory. By then, Thatcher was firmly in control. Party officials say he campaigned almost independently of the party organization, promising more prosperity and good government. To NDP charges that the Liberals were giving away the resources of the province to foreign capitalists, Thatcher argued the province was getting jobs and good times out of the deal and investment was necessary. He painted the NDP as simply the mouthpiece of international labor organizations.

In Prince Albert, Steuart responded to the NDP charges with a typical burst of rhetoric. To the complaint that Liberal resource policies meant selling out the province, he replied: "Under the socialists, they couldn't give the province away." He argued that Liberal policies were transforming Saskatchewan into an economic power. "Saskatchewan residents are no longer the stubble jumping clodhoppers of Canada as we were previously portrayed. We are proud of our province, of its rising place in the nation and our chests are out. You ain't seen nothing yet." As if to support the claims of prosperity, federal officials let it be known Saskatchewan would soon pass from the status of "have not" to "have" and equalization payments would stop.

Considering his high expectations, the election did not turn out well for Thatcher. The Liberals were returned with an increased majority, winning thirty-five seats to the NDP's twenty-four. But the Liberal share of the popular vote — 45.6 percent — was just 1.3 percent higher than the NDP vote. Several cabinet ministers had also been defeated. A quiet side-issue of election night was that the PCs lost their one Legislature seat in Arm River and the party's share of the popular vote declined by almost half to 9.8 percent.

It was, for Thatcher, a setback in the guise of victory. "He was shocked on election night," said a party official who spent part of the evening with the premier. "He thought he was going to bury the socialists."

October 11, 1967, marked a turning point for the Thatcher government. Liberal MLAs say the mood inside the government and party changed almost overnight from optimism and buoyant predictions to grim determination and a survivor mentality. "Overnight, we went from being benign to being repressive," says a former caucus member. "Most of it dealt with economics."

There are several schools of thought about the reason for the change of mood. Some in the party argue Thatcher was angry that the voters had not given him a bigger majority after his efforts. He decided to get even. Others argue Thatcher saw the approaching economic downturn of the late sixties and began to take steps early to tighten down the economy. This explanation does not account for the lack of warning in the 1967 campaign and the promise of better times.

Whatever the explanation, the change in mood came quickly. Steuart recalls a cabinet meeting on October 12, the day after the election, when Thatcher told his ministers there would have to be cutbacks. "After all the talk of good times, I was astounded," says then Deputy Premier Steuart, the man considered one of Thatcher's closest contacts. The next day, Thatcher announced the age of austerity had arrived. "We went downhill after that," says Steuart. "He became obsessed with controlling government spending."

The result was a series of confrontations with various groups in the province, confrontations which gradually alienated the public and eroded public support. First, Thatcher convinced the Liberal executive to postpone the annual convention with the argument the party was exhausted after fighting an election. Some party critics saw it as a way to avoid internal fights over the austerity and a move by the leader to dominate the executive. Then began the public fights. Thatcher started a dispute with the university community when he told them university spending would have to be more carefully controlled. That was followed by fights with teachers over an imposed 6 percent salary increase limit and an order to increase pupil-teacher ratios.

There were other disputes with hotel keepers, public servants, labor unions, and federal Liberals. The objective of the government's general policy was to cut back costs, save money, and prepare for the worst.

By March 1, 1968, Thatcher had decided even greater restraints were needed on the economy, and a budget presented that day in the Legislature by newly-appointed Finance Minister Steuart was the vehicle used to announce the bad news. Scores of taxes were raised; utilization fees of $2.50 per day on hospital use and $1.50 for a visit to the doctor were imposed on health care services; sales taxes, gasoline taxes, and liquor prices were all raised. The increases would raise an additional $30 million in a budget of $338.4 million.

The bad news was accompanied by a lecture from Steuart about rising health and education costs and abuse of the health care system by the public. He said the government needed more revenue, and rather than deficit budget, borrow, or cut back services, tax increases had been authorized.

It was a difficult time for Steuart. The budget had been largely prepared by Thatcher before Steuart was appointed finance minister, and he was called upon simply to announce the details and share the backlash. In caucus, Steuart said later, he had not opposed the tax increase proposals, and although he had argued against utilization fees and the political problems they would create, he had not made a strong point of it. Publicly, he defined and defended the moves. "This is the most difficult and probably the most unpopular alternative but I'm convinced it is the responsible and proper course to take at this time," he said in the Legislature.

He was right about the "unpopular" part. The NDP immediately dubbed it "Black Friday" (a steal from the federal PCs who used the same label to describe the day twelve years earlier when Louis St. Laurent's Liberals imposed closure in the pipeline debate). They blasted the Liberals for taxing the sick through deterrent fees and for creating unemployment and hardship through repressive and regressive taxation.

However, while the NDP led an effective mobilization of opposition to the government after the budget, many groups in the province needed little urging. Farmers were angry because the tax on farm-used gasoline was increased; consumers were angry because taxes were higher on most purchases; students, teachers, and school administration officials were angry because of tight guidelines and what they considered to be excessive government interference in their affairs. By the spring of 1968, the glow of victory from the previous fall had disappeared.

By then, the economy was also beginning to turn down, and although the effects would be more severe in 1969 and 1970, wheat prices were already beginning to drop, potash prices and markets were getting soft, and unemployment was rising.

Through Liberal eyes, there was one major economic success story to be promoted, however. In October 1968, Premier Thatcher travelled to Prince Albert to officially open the Prince Albert Pulp Company mill, and he offered it as an example of the jobs and development which a Liberal government could attract to Saskatchewan. More such mills should be opened in the north, he said, and "the only complaint we have about American capital is that we aren't getting enough of it." The government quickly began negotiating details for more pulp mill developments, and Thatcher warned striking unions that if they delayed development in the north, he would pass legislation to keep them on the job.

Thatcher's triumphant day in Prince Albert was the result of more than three years of work and negotiations. The major government figure behind the venture was Dave Steuart. The idea of building a pulp mill in Prince Albert, a small city perched on the edge of the northern Saskatchewan tree belt, had long been a dream of both CCF and Liberal politicians. When the Liberals were elected to power, they made it clear the government would like to see that dream translated into some dollars invested and jobs created. New York capitalist Karl Landegger, president of Parsons and Whittemore was interested, and Steuart was designated the government representative to negotiate the deal.

In many ways, it was an unequal match. Steuart was a small-town politician anxious to attract development to his Prince Albert constituency and often in awe of the man across the bargaining table. Landegger was a freewheeling operator with worldwide financial interests, an eye for making money, and the corporate power to strike a hard bargain with a provincial government anxious to attract development and prove to its critics that private enterprise was the way to go. In private, he also had a surprising tendency to sound liberal. He could spend the day trying to squeeze every conceivable concession out of the government and to ensure maximum freedom of operation for his company and then at night over a drink surprise his opponents with a strong defense of government social programs and high death duties to reduce the possibility of inherited privilege.

As negotiations between Landegger and Steuart began, relations were uncertain, and at one point Landegger asked Thatcher to appoint a new negotiator because he did not take Steuart seriously. Thatcher refused, negotiations continued, and in time, Steuart and Landegger struck a deal and became friends.

The deal was announced in late 1965. A $65-million bleached kraft pulp mill would be built in the city, and counting mill workers, bush employment, and spin-off, 5,000 jobs would be created. The deal was a mixture of private investment and public concession. To attract the huge company into the province, the government agreed to provide a loan guarantee and some services in return for 30 percent of the equity. The company was granted cutting rights to 18,000 square miles of timber, and a Crown corporation, Saskatchewan Forest Products, would supply wood for the first four years.

When the plant opened in 1968, the government made it the centrepiece of its industrial strategy, despite complaints by the NDP and some labor groups that the province had given the New York partners too many capital, services, and timber rights concessions.

But economic conditions continued to deteriorate and Thatcher's attempts to lay some of the blame on Ottawa and the "fuzzy headed thinkers" in the federal Liberal party did nothing to ease the problems. Unemployment grew, the potash industry was in danger of collapse because of poor prices and industry overbuilding, and large grain harvests left prices low and granaries full. In 1969, Thatcher intervened in the potash industry with production controls and a floor price.[1] In 1970, Steuart presented the first deficit budget in almost a decade, while health and education costs continued to climb.

The government attempted to counterattack on February 18, 1970, when it announced another deal with Parsons and Whittemore for construction of a pulp mill at Meadow Lake in northwestern Saskatchewan. Again, it would be a combination of private and public ownership, and

---

[1] The move was challenged in court by Central Canada Potash Company, and late in 1978, the Supreme Court of Canada ruled Thatcher had exceeded his constitutional jurisdiction by interfering with interprovincial trade and commerce.

along with loan guarantees and infrastructure, the government was granting the company cutting rights to huge tracts of northern bushland. The majority of shares in the Athabasca pulp mill would be owned by Parsons and Whittemore, with the government a minority shareholder. In the Legislature, Thatcher credited Steuart with yet another triumph for the Liberal vision of the future: "I cannot pay too much tribute to his work," said the premier. "It was outstanding."

The assessment was not universally accepted. The NDP Opposition again launched an attack on the scheme, and this time the criticism found some eager listeners. The campaign of criticism centred on the charge that the Athabasca plan was a sell-out of provincial resources to the multinational capitalist friends of the Liberals. While the government talked about investment and jobs created, the NDP complained about huge tracts of land given up to company use, the concessions to a huge company which hardly needed financial help, and the subsidies offered by the government for just 30 percent of the ownership. It was, they said, another case of the public sector taking the risks and the private sector getting the rewards. As an example of the "bad deal" negotiated by Steuart, opponents pointed out that the government had agreed to supply wood to the Prince Albert operation at a loss for the first few years as a way to help the mill get off the ground.

Even the pro-business *Financial Post* ventured the opinion that the deal "appeared rather favorable to the private partner in the mill."

Clearly, Thatcher's ideal of a new prosperity built on eye-catching developments was no longer a salable dream.

The deterioration in the economy and political fortunes of the party was matched by Thatcher's increasingly autocratic control over the party. Liberal officials say in the latter years of the sixties the leader paid little attention to the party. "The Liberal Party was Ross Thatcher's fief," says former party secretary Roy Currie of Saskatoon.

At the time, this appeared to be the least of the party's worries. Dissent about Thatcher's power or attitudes was rarely heard, although dissidents complained privately (and later, when it was safer) that the leader acted without consulting the party, that he manipulated conventions to make sure his supporters were elected to the executive, and that he gave the party little role in formulating policy. At the time, there was little outcry, and Steuart says within caucus and cabinet there was virtually no opposition because most believed in Thatcher or felt his basic policies were correct. They were becoming increasingly out of touch with the public mood. "You look back and say maybe you should have done something but at the time it didn't look so bad," Steuart said in a later interview. "We were in power. It's the nature of the beast."

A disenchanted backbench MLA suggests it resulted from the type of people surrounding Thatcher. "One of the requirements of a cabinet minister in those days was to be able to say 'yes, yes, yes' and to say no more," he said in a 1978 interview.

When there were attempts to stand up to the leader or to the prevalent policy, they were quickly quashed. Rosetown MLA George Leith showed a rare fit of independence when he spoke against antilabor legislation in caucus and later publicly refused to endorse the government's policy at a convention. He was ostracized by party leaders. Similarly, provincial Liberals who wanted to actively support the federal Liberal cause found themselves on the outside, meeting privately on Saturday mornings because they felt there was no place for them in the provincial party.

Steuart says that during those years Thatcher also became increasingly jealous of any perceived threats to his dominance. When Steuart represented Saskatchewan at a federal-provincial first ministers' conference in Ottawa in 1969, for instance, he received favorable Ontario press coverage, both for his wit and for his tough statements about federal Liberal policies. He says when he returned to Regina, Thatcher made it clear he did not like the grandstanding.

The 1971 pre-election budget was a show of Liberal largesse. There were no tax increases in the $450 million package but there were promises of more jobs, efforts to keep the environment clean, and grants to homeowners and businesses. The election was called for June 23, and in the weeks before the vote, there was another flurry of promises. Although some cabinet members felt Thatcher was still concerned about an impending depression and another Liberal victory would have meant more austerity, the campaign featured promises of more development. It was also a campaign based on a defense of the Liberal record and warnings about a slowdown in development if the NDP won. The Liberals were promoting labor courts as a way to bring labor peace to the province.

In contrast, the NDP led by lawyer Allan Blakeney was blaming the Liberals for a deterioration in health care and education, for making a gift of the province's resources to their "corporate friends," and for following a policy of harsh economic restraint when the provincial economy needed some leadership from the government.

Although Liberal leaders began the campaign feeling they could pull off a win if the party could get the message out that it had been fiscally responsible at a time when hard decisions were necessary, many began to doubt the outcome as the campaign progressed. Signs began to surface that the NDP campaign, with its flashy program "New Deal for People" and a new, energetic leader, was catching on. The NDP promised expanded government programs, an end to "give-aways" to outside capitalists, and strong leadership.

Some Liberal front-runners, like Steuart, began to see the government campaign as superficially exciting but basically shallow. He and other party leaders began to worry that the frantic campaigning pace would not overcome the voter hostility built up over the previous three years. "The election was unreal," Steuart said later. "It was like a dance without partners. We were just going through the motions."

In late May, John Diefenbaker's brother Elmer died, and Steuart attended the funeral in Saskatoon. He says Diefenbaker predicted a Liberal loss. "When I told Ross, I think it was the first time he really began to worry."

During the campaign, Thatcher's health was also deteriorating, and as the campaign drew to a close, the leader was tiring and his tactics became more frantic.[2] His speeches were more liberally spiced with antisocialist rhetoric and less with positive campaigning.

Election night proved Diefenbaker right. The NDP was swept into power with 55 percent of the popular vote and forty-five of sixty Legislature seats. The Liberals dropped from thirty-four to fifteen seats with 43 percent of the vote. The Conservatives collapsed to just 2 percent. In fact, the Liberals had held their own in the vote count. The 1971 vote total was just seven fewer than the party had received in 1967. However, the number of voters had expanded, and virtually all the PC vote went NDP.

Despite an electoral boundary redrawing which heavily favored the Liberals, their territory shrank to a few city seats in Regina, some small towns like Rosthern and Meadow Lake, and the traditional right-wing rural vote in the southeast. The NDP, despite a decidedly leftward swing in policies and image through the influence of the radical Waffle group, had captured many traditional Liberal areas and won a clean sweep in Saskatoon.

The NDP victory was in part due to the unpopularity of Liberal policies and the personality of Premier Thatcher. But it could also be partly explained in the shift of the Saskatchewan voting population from rural to urban, old to young. The NDP attracted the newly-enfranchised young (the voting age had been lowered to eighteen for the first time), the left-leaning, and the growing urban middle-class and professional groups with a program of more active government, greater provincial control over resource exploitation, and a land bank scheme of government-owned and leased land to help young people into farming.

Liberal strength had been reduced to some traditional bases — pockets of rural conservatism, longstanding professional groups such as doctors, and the business community.

If the party were to rise from defeat, a rebuilding program would be necessary.

---

[2] Thatcher suffered from chronic diabetes and required medication throughout the campaign.

Chapter Three

THE STEUART YEARS BEGIN

The days of late June 1971 were a melancholy time for Saskatchewan Liberals. Most had misread the signs of voter unrest and, consequently, the election result. Defeat came as a surprise. The scope of defeat came as a shock.

After seven years of power, the party had been overwhelmingly rejected by the voters. Its dreams of an industrialized Saskatchewan free of "socialism" lay in tatters, spurned by the people it was meant to help. In Regina, members of the cabinet began clearing their desks in preparation for the new, victorious tenants. Treasurer Steuart said the sudden change in status became apparent to him quickly during those quiet Regina days. "Before the election, my office was always humming, phones ringing, bond dealers and road contractors coming around to talk. Then came the election. It was like the curtain dropped. There was nobody. I even checked the phone to make sure it wasn't disconnected."

In the country, MLAs and defeated candidates reported their supporters were in shock. "They just couldn't believe we had lost," said one.

Two questions were to dominate post-election Liberal talk. What happened, and what was the future of Ross Thatcher's leadership? Party leaders were uneasily awaiting the inevitable day when fingers would start to point and blame would be laid, usually at someone else's feet.

There was no shortage of theories to account for the Liberals' defeat. The government's economic measures had been too drastic and repressive; it had alienated key groups such as teachers, unionists, civil servants; the government's attitude to the electorate was arrogant and out-of-touch; federal policies and the depressed economy had damaged government efforts; and the fabled Liberal organization had not been successful in getting the vote out.

Several months later, Steuart coined a phrase which would often be repeated to describe the provincial Liberal role in their own defeat: "We made too many enemies during our term in office," he said. "If we missed making enemies of anyone, it was because we hadn't met them."

On the question of leadership, Thatcher moved quickly to clear up some of the confusion. He called a meeting of caucus and the executive soon after the election and took full responsibility for the defeat. He also proposed to resign from the leadership, but according to some participants in the closed meeting, he suggested it would be better for the party if he stayed on as leader until after the special summer session the new government was planning to call to implement some of its election promises. There was little opposition to the ideas from those present and little attempt to gang up on Thatcher or any of the senior party officials for the defeat. However, there was one brief but bitter flare-up at the meeting. Former Legislature Speaker Jim Snedker was the first to speak after Thatcher, offering a fiery speech which called for some party housecleaning, beginning at the top. Before anyone else got involved, Steuart jumped to his feet and attacked Snedker. The outburst was intimidating, and the dicusssion did not get much further.

That meeting seemed to settle the leadership question for the moment and party leaders began preparing for the special session, called to begin in early August. Although there were several in the caucus who were ambitious for the leader's job, they were not willing to begin their campaigns until it became clear what Thatcher's intentions were. In fact, there was a growing feeling within the party during July that he might decide to remain as leader, despite his commitment to leave. It would depend, the corridor talk went, on how well he performed as leader during the special session and how party regulars reacted to him in the months ahead.

Since the voters appeared to be reacting to his attitudes as much as his policies, it would have required some dramatic changes in the head-strong leader. But many in the party were not ruling it out. During the last years of government and the strenuous last election campaign, his health had taken a beating, but as the weeks went by, associates reported his spirits were climbing and his health appeared to be improving. In the late afternoon of July 23, a month after the election defeat, Thatcher and some of his advisors and political friends met in his Opposition Leader's office to swap stories about their days in government. They reported later his mood had been buoyant. He was looking forward to tangling with the men who had inherited his government machinery.

Late that night, word flashed from his home that Ross Thatcher had died of a heart attack at the age of fifty-four.

The party and the province were stunned. The province had lost a man who had dominated its political stage for more than a decade. He had been loved and hated with equal passion — few were indifferent.

The party had lost more than just a leader. In the twelve years since he had taken over as leader, he had made the party almost totally dependent on him. He controlled the policy, the money, the spirit. He had created it, defined it, and then almost destroyed it. Now at a time when the party needed inspiration and leadership, it was left with a suddenly-created vacuum. To make matters worse, it also lacked a president. Former president Bobby Thompson had drowned weeks earlier during the campaign.

In the aftermath of Thatcher's death, tributes flowed in from both friends and foes. Many of them, in paying tribute to Thatcher's contribution to the Liberal party and his strength, put the party's leadership problems into sharp focus. "As we look for his intellectual and spiritual successor, we sadly realize he was irreplaceable," said the conservative publication *Canada Month* in the most cutting comment. "He was the only leader in the history of Canadian politics to have resisted and turned back for a time the dominant spirit of our weakening age. In that, he was unique."

Despite the blow of Thatcher's death, the Liberal caucus decided to carry on with the special Legislature session beginning in a few days. Party leaders decided it was important to show members and the voting public that the Liberal party was still alive and vigorous. The fourteen MLAs led by recently-appointed Acting House Leader Dave Steuart went into the session prepared to do battle.

"I promise you, Mr. Premier and your forty-five members, as well as the people of Saskatchewan, that this small band of fourteen Liberal members will work and fight and grow just as we did in 1960, 1961 and 1962 and when we finally defeated you in 1964," Steuart said in his opening speech during Throne Speech debate. "We don't have another Ross Thatcher on this side of the House, but we have his memory, his example and we have fourteen enthusiastic members who have dedicated themselves to give this government the most responsible and toughest opposition ever seen in Saskatchewan."

Bravado aside, the scene as the Legislature opened was a depressing one for Liberals. The magnitude of their defeat was obvious as MLAs, members of their families, provincial Queen's Bench judges, and several hundred invited guests gathered to listen to the new government's first, brief Throne Speech. The tired, aging, demoralized Liberal caucus faced a government caucus three times its size and brimming with promise, enthusiasm, and smugness.

The star was clearly Allan Blakeney, a slim, youthful-looking forty-five-year-old who had been elected leader the year before in a bitter convention dominated by a sharp split between right and left ideologies. Blakeney was solid party establishment but he also projected a public image of a thoughtful, trustworthy progressive. He grew up in a solidly Conservative Nova Scotia setting but fell under the intellectual influence of both the CCF and the cooperative Antigonish Movement during his years at the Dalhousie University Law School. He was a Rhodes Scholar who travelled west to Saskatchewan to become an influential civil servant in the 1950s Douglas government and later to practice law in Regina. In 1960, he was elected to the legislature and quickly joined the cabinet as health and later finance minister. As health minister, he helped usher in the age of medicare.

In Opposition, during the leadership convention, and later in government, Blakeney proved himself an able political infighter. But he was widely seen publicly as a man above politics, a statesman well suited to projecting the new image of a progressive Saskatchewan to the world. He was without intellectual equal in the Legislature. He was a sharp debater, a good campaigner, and a leader widely respected for his image and style.

Surrounding Blakeney in the inner circle of powerful cabinet ministers was a group of men who also appeared to hold much promise in those halcyon days of the new government: Saskatoon lawyer Roy Romanow, deputy premier, house leader, and attorney-general who would become a master politician; Tisdale farmer Jack Messer, a wealthy and aggressive agriculture minister who would spearhead some radical changes in agriculture policy; Gordon MacMurchy, a slow-moving farmer and small-town politician who took on the education portfolio and soon became a leader of the right-wing faction in the government; Walter Smishek, a Regina labor organizer who led the government into some popular and costly expansions of the health care system; and Biggar schoolteacher Elwood Cowley, a bright, talented, congenial man who would figure prominently in many of the government's major policy and political decisions.

The government went into the special summer session intent on quick passage of several major election promises. The Liberals under Steuart showed themselves ready to fight, at least with words, during the nine-day session. But the Liberal caucus also proved it had yet to learn the lessons of June 23. Although they bowed to the electorate and sided with the government in repealing utilization fees for medicare users, Opposition MLAs strongly opposed the government's decision to repeal the unpopular antilabor Bill 2 which allowed the outlawing of strikes in essential services. Steuart argued it was the first example of the "labor bosses" collecting their IOUs from the NDP and he predicted it would lead to "irresponsible" actions by labor.

When Premier Blakeney announced the government was cancelling the plan for development of the Athabasca Pulp Mill near Meadow Lake, Steuart charged it was an example of the NDP being dominated by the Waffle, which he considered "far left socialists" and communists.

And when the NDP introduced and subsequently passed the Family Farm Protection Act, giving farmers a year's moratorium on repayment if they owed money on land, machinery, or livestock, the Liberals complained that it would hurt the credit chances of farmers in the future. Steuart suggested the government offer loan guarantees instead so the financial institutions would get their money. Although the NDP majority got its way and passed the bill, Steuart and the Liberals tried a "mini-filibuster" to try to delay passage until more of the groups affected were heard from on the issue.

It was a spirited effort by the recently-beaten Liberals, but in view of the economic plight of many Saskatchewan farmers after several years of low prices and financial losses, it was hardly a vote-grabber. The Liberals showed they were still alive, but they had some lessons to learn in populist politics.

While the battle for public credibility was being waged noisily in the Legislature, a battle for future control of the Liberal party was quietly shaping up behind the scenes. Although it would be almost two months before the first candidate for leadership would formally announce his intentions, campaign strategies and allegiances began to form within days of Thatcher's death.

The first job for Thatcher's heirs was to consider the state of the party they were inheriting. On a superficial first glance, they found things surprisingly sound. While party strength in the Legislature had been reduced to just fourteen members, the Liberal vote in the election had been just a handful shy of the 1967 election-winning total. Although the NDP picked up the former Conservative votes and the new voters, Liberal popular strength had remained solid at 43 percent. The Liberals also claimed 41,000 signed-up members in that election year and they remained the only alternative to the NDP. Finally, money appeared to be no object in the fight which lay ahead. In addition to the party's well-developed ability to raise funds inside and outside the province, Liberal officials found $935,000 in the party coffers after Thatcher's death, according to party sources.[1]

This relatively healthy state of affairs, combined with the wide-spread party belief that the voter decision was just a diversion which would be corrected as soon as people saw the "socialists" in action, made the party leadership a desirable commodity.

While Thatcher was alive, many in the party considered Welfare Minister Cy MacDonald his likely successor. He shared many of Thatcher's conservative philosophies and, although not as popular, powerful, or high profile as Steuart, he was younger and considered more independent of Thatcher's image.

"Many in the party didn't consider Steuart a likely candidate," MLA Don Macdonald of Moose Jaw said later. "He came with Ross and he'd go with Ross."

Steuart had other ideas. During July, he says, he decided Thatcher

---

[1] Party officials have been defensive about this and the total in the "kitty" left by Thatcher was never officially disclosed. After Thatcher's death, an audit committee was established within the party to find out if a proper, audited accounting of party reserves was in place. It later announced that the books were in order. Thatcher had been the only person completely aware of the financial picture and the reserve was found securely in bank accounts and investment certificates.

would likely not retire. He was not about to challenge his mentor. But when the leader died, the picture changed. "The day he died, I decided to run," he said. The only question then was how to overcome his handicaps, cash in on his strengths and debts, and outmanoeuvre his opponents. Steuart turned out to be adept at the game. By September 17 when he became the first candidate to announce officially that he was running for the leadership, he had already virtually wrapped up the victory. In the process, he had become more liberal-sounding than ever before, more flexible than many thought possible, further removed from Thatcher and his policies than many thought honest.

However, in the immediate aftermath of Thatcher's death, it was far from clear that Steuart would become leader, or that he even wanted the job. Leadership speculation centred around MacDonald, former Education Minister Cliff McIsaac from North Battleford, and occasionally, newcomer MLA Ken MacLeod, a Regina lawyer. Only the hometown *Prince Albert Daily Herald* was publicly touting Steuart as a successor, and on July 26 it fretted editorially about a news story from Saskatoon which quoted Steuart as saying he wasn't interested in the job.

The very next day, Steuart made the first of several sly moves he was later to credit with winning him the leadership. With a Legislature session looming, Steuart called a Liberal caucus meeting. As deputy premier in the former government, no one questioned his right to call a meeting and all MLAs showed up in Regina. Steuart realized if he could convince fellow MLAs to elect him caucus chairman, it would give him a summer platform while his competitors were scrambling for attention.

Shortly before caucus began meeting, he suggested to former cabinet colleague Dave Boldt of Rosthern that the caucus would need a chairman. Boldt told Steuart it should be him and Steuart quickly replied: "If you think I should be it, nominate me." Boldt did, and with Steuart leaving the impression he was not in the running for permanent leader, no one opposed him. The caucus announced Steuart had been unanimously chosen caucus chairman and House leader for the summer session. It was victory number one for the candidate.

"I told Cy later the leadership race was over that day," Steuart recalled later to an interviewer. "By the time his forces got it together, it was too late." MacDonald later realized his mistake. "That gave Dave the platform and the leadership," he said. During the caucus vote, MacDonald had supported the motion because he felt Steuart was the best-liked Liberal and most fiery debater at a time when the party needed a morale boost. "The caucus wanted to go into that session with fire and Dave would give it to us," he said. Besides, MacDonald didn't consider Steuart a serious threat to his own leadership ambitions.

Steuart's next move illustrated how naive MacDonald had been. Although House leader and caucus chairman positions gave him a platform, there was one more title Steuart wanted in order to make his ambitions secure. At a summer executive meeting, he proposed the party add "acting leader" to his titles. By then, MacDonald's forces were mobilizing and they were wise to their competitor's campaigning skills. Several of MacDonald's supporters on the executive argued against Steuart's proposal, and when Senator Herb Sparrow from North Battleford, a former party president, began to dispute the wisdom of the move, Steuart sensed some executive members were being swayed. He won his point with an emotional speech charging the party would look weak and disorganized if it did not show enough confidence in its House leader to make him "acting leader" as well. The vote was won, and the next day provincial council ratified it. Steuart was officially the acting leader and he felt he was in the driver's seat.

When the Legislature session ended in mid-August, campaigning for the leadership began in earnest. The convention was scheduled for December in Saskatoon. The leadership vote would be December 11.[2]

By then, three candidates had emerged — Steuart, MacDonald, and unexpected dark-horse entry George Leith from Rosetown, a farmer and seven-year MLA who had been defeated June 23.[3]

In style, image, and platform, party members were being offered a clear choice for their next leader.

Steuart, at fifty-five, was the oldest. After six years as deputy premier and twelve years as a close associate of Thatcher, he was the establishment candidate. It was assumed that as one of the chief architects of former Liberal government policy, his election would provide no real break with the past. Yet his reputation as a conciliator made him a likely candidate to heal the rifts which had grown in the party, both left against right and federal against provincial. He also had a reputation as an excellent organizer.

MacDonald was the youngest at forty-three. He was handsome, had a reputation for competence as welfare minister in the Thatcher government, and of the three, he appeared most likely to be the "media personality" many felt would be needed to counter the high-profile Blakeney. He had earned a reputation for conservative thinking, both as a teacher at the well-known Notre Dame College in Wilcox, Saskatchewan, and as welfare minister. Yet many felt he would promote and implement those conserva-

---

[2] An attempt by Lumsden MLA Gary Lane to have the convention delayed for two years while the newer MLAs had a chance to prove themselves was unsuccessful. He put his idea forward at an October party executive meeting in Weyburn, arguing Steuart should be interim leader but perhaps a new face was needed as a permanent leader. Many executive members felt Lane was primarily interested in the job himself and although he disclaimed any intention of running for leader if the convention was delayed, the idea was turned down. Lane then publicly supported Steuart.

[3] Lawyer Ken MacLeod actually did consider running for the leadership but Steuart called him into his office during the summer and told him support for the Steuart campaign already evident in the constituencies and caucus could not be overtaken. MacLeod was convinced and subsequently publicly endorsed Steuart for leader.

tive ideals without alienating the groups which had been alienated by Thatcher's arrogant actions and insensitive politicking.

Leith was the unknown. He had been a backbencher throughout the Thatcher government, and his one brief bout of publicity came when he publicly criticized his own government for its antilabor stances — the only Liberal MLA to do so. The action, as well as his identification with some federal Liberal ideas, led to his reputation as a principled outsider. He ran an antiestablishment campaign which attracted many of the young idealists in the party.

The leadership campaigning took the candidates around the province to address prospective delegates. As the debate wore on, it produced some strange twists. MacDonald failed to excite and, coupled with his failure to present the new approach to conservative politics which many supporters hoped for, he was politically outclassed by Steuart and his workers. Leith was never a serious threat, but as he campaigned for a more open party, greater membership involvement in party affairs, and a more tolerant attitude toward Thatcher enemies ranging from organized labor to federal Liberals, he forced the other candidates to respond to his issues.

Finally, it was Steuart who dominated the campaign. Surprisingly, he also became the spokesman for change, sensing in the membership a mood receptive to the changes which Leith called for and promising to deliver better than Leith could. His policy positions moderated as he preached the need to "open the party up," involve more people in decision-making, and find some common ground with groups which had left the Liberals. He shied away from labelling himself simply a free enterpriser and called for a mix of public and private enterprise with the emphasis on private initiative whenever possible. Instead of attacking welfare freeloaders, he said he supported a guaranteed government job program to get people off welfare and into the work force. He promised to keep the organizational structure of the party strong and to try to patch things up with the federal Liberals.

While proclaiming that the achievements of the Thatcher government would live on, he also worked hard to dissociate himself from some of the government's excesses and failures. He told one interviewer he would not be an image of Ross Thatcher and, while they had shared some philosophies, their approaches and styles were different. "I was a contrast to him and he wanted it that way."

Of course, Steuart wasn't depending on his speeches and change of emphasis to win the election for him. Although he went into the convention well ahead of the other two candidates, Steuart workers also told delegates who seemed uncertain because of his age or close assocation with Thatcher that Steuart would be an interim leader, holding the party together and maintaining its voter base until a new leader came along who would lead it to victory. Steuart denies that was an official part of his campaign, but he says it was a tactic adopted by some. "We didn't use it officially, but I'm sure it was used." Others say it was an important part of the pitch made by Steuart workers to the wavering delegates.

However, many obviously voted for Steuart because they believed in him and felt he could lead the party back to glory. On the first ballot on that hot afternoon at the Saskatoon Centennial Auditorium, Steuart led the polls with 404 votes. MacDonald trailed with 295 and Leith picked up 171. The second ballot tally was Steuart, 535; MacDonald, 314.

It was an impressive victory. The defeated candidates quickly made it plain they wanted the party to stay united, although some of Leith's supporters privately were bitter that more of the relatively small federal faction at the convention did not support him. There were rumors that Steuart had made a deal with federal Wheat Board Minister Otto Lang, Saskatchewan's cabinet representative, to heal the federal-provincial breach in return for federal support in the vote. Such a formal deal is unlikely nor was it necessary. The federalists at the convention split their vote, but the majority supported Steuart because they felt Steuart was the best bet to beat Blakeney and because even at the height of federal-provincial feuding, he had been a good contact. Steuart campaigned on a platform of uniting the party, and they believed him.

Along with a new leader, party delegates, unaccustomed to exercising internal levers of power, found themselves electing a new executive. Under Thatcher, the executive had been dominated by people who tended to rubber-stamp his decisions. They made few demands for real power, and little power rested with them. The 1971 convention, with the winds of change blowing around the hall, was quite a different scene. Most positions on the executive were contested, and many of the candidates promoted themselves as people anxious to make the executive a body that mattered. The key position of president went to Regina lawyer Garry Wilson, a member of the Liberal establishment and a long-established Saskatchewan political family. Like Steuart, one of his winning campaign pledges was an opening up of the party structure to permit, even encourage, more membership voice in how it was run and what it said.

The party emerged from the convention appearing united and enthusiastic (helped in part by the November by-election of farmer Jack Wiebe in Ross Thatcher's Morse riding). Steuart was the tenth leader in the party's sixty-six-year history and the first Roman Catholic to hold the position.

Judging from the media editorial opinion which followed the victory, Steuart was expected to be combative, a tough political opponent for the new government, and more flexible than Thatcher in his opinions. There also seemed to be a consensus (based in part on pledges by the candidates during the race) that he would have just one chance to get the party back into power.

"There is little doubt that the new leader will only have one crack at the leadership," editorialized the *Prince Albert Daily Herald*. "If he fails in 1975, he will probably be forced to step down."

If Steuart was feeling any pressure from that ultimatum, he wasn't showing it. The new leader quickly set out a number of goals for himself and the party in the years ahead. He told a victory party the Liberals should dedicate themselves to closing the gap "between the haves and the have-nots." He told a news conference he felt the message from delegates was that the party should become more moderate in its policies, "They thought we were a little right of centre and they wanted us to move over a little to the left." Steuart, for years the single-minded crusader against the left, said he was prepared to do that. He wanted to tap the "grass roots" of the party for ideas, workers, and inspiration. He would follow the wishes of the party and respond to some of the concerns the Leith campaign had pointed out.[4]

But first there was a federal election on the horizon, and for the first time in a decade, the new leader pledged the provincial party would do all it could to elect federal Liberals in the province. He said the party's first responsibility was "to get behind Otto Lang and give him 12 members in the next federal election."

Then, having laid down some directions and raised some expectations, Steuart left the province for a long-awaited rest in the southern sun.

---

[4] Leith supporters were not about to let him forget that promise. They formed an informal grouping within the party known as the "171 Club," a name drawn from the number of first-ballot votes Leith had drawn. Members of this group would play a prominent role during the next four years, trying to fulfil the promise of creating a more moderate, accountable party.

Chapter Four

A PARTY MAN AS LEADER

The man who emerged from the convention as leader was in many ways a strange choice, considering the job of rejuvenation and change which lay ahead.

He was very much a Thatcher Liberal who had helped both create and then vigorously defend the policies and attitudes of the discredited government. He was a gut conservative at a time when the voters were leaning left. He was fifty-five years old and a twenty-year veteran of politics when the trend was towards youth.

He was also a politician with an uncertain public acceptance in his home riding. After failing in his first attempt at winning a seat in Prince Albert in 1960, he swept into office with a 2,500 vote margin in a by-election two years later. After that, each election became a fight. In 1964, the victory margin was 78 votes. In 1967, it was 169 votes, and in 1971, he withstood the NDP sweep with a 44-vote victory which was confirmed only after a recount. Steuart and his supporters made light of the close electoral margins, dubbing him "landslide Dave." But a leader who does not have a strong home base which allows him to campaign across the province is of dubious value.

Still, he was Dave Steuart — respected in the party for his hard work, capable of flexibility when the mood was changing, astute in the ways of political manoeuvring and one of the best campaigners in the province.

He was more complex and intelligent than his detractors would admit; more vulnerable and uncertain than his "hatchet man" history would suggest; and more cunning and ambitious than his "nice guy" image appeared.

Steuart was a creation of both his past and his ambition. His upbringing and experience made him a conservative who leaned liberal. His political ambition and a genuine tinge of liberal concern for the less fortunate allowed him to be a moderate when the time was right.

Above all, Dave Steuart was a political animal.

He was born in Moose Jaw, Saskatchewan, on January 26, 1916, the son of businessman F. J. Steuart. The senior Mr. Steuart instilled in his four sons a feeling of his own pride in self-reliance and initiative. It included a strong dislike of government.

"He always said you'd be better off owning a peanut stand than working for the government," Steuart recalls.

His early years were relatively uneventful, peaceful, and middle-class. But 1928 and the approaching depression changed that scenario. His father went bankrupt selling cars, and the family moved from Moose Jaw to Regina, thirty-eight miles east, where Steuart senior became a store clerk and the Steuart home took in boarders to help pay the rent. Later his father became a travelling salesman, and young Dave took a job delivering newspapers.

Steuart later remembered them as basically happy days, and the father's resolve to survive the hard times without looking for government relief impressed his son. "Dad's example rubbed off on me. It had to."

By 1933, the Depression and drought were in full force in Saskatchewan, and seventeen-year-old Dave decided it was time to move west in search of prosperity. He hitchhiked to Calgary and then, with a friend, rode the rails to Vancouver. A letter of introduction from home and some aggressive self-promotion landed him a job with the Canadian Western Lumber Company in New Westminister. The job would prove to be a harsh introduction to the world of the workplace, labor agitation, and politics.

The British Columbia which presented itself to Steuart was an unsettled place — a land of unemployment, recently-created work camps for the unemployed, poor working conditions for those lucky enough to have a job, vigorous organizing efforts by several unions, and repressive measures by employers to keep the unions out.

The Fraser Mills lumber company where Steuart found work, was no exception. A strike by the International Woodworkers of America had recently been broken and the company was tense. Union organizers were active among the workers. Company officials were watching, ready to stamp out any signs of renewed union strength.

Steuart said later it was his first contact with unions and he didn't like what he saw. He refused to support the union and remained largely outside the debate, earning his ten dollars a week and trying to have a good time. Steuart said he found the union dominated by communists intent on using the organization to attack the economic system.

"The program they had wasn't 'let a union in and we'll do something for you.' It was 'get into a union and overthrow the system.' "

It wasn't a perception which attracted Steuart. He said he was aware of poor working conditions (worse for immigrant workers than those of British descent, since they were paid less, had to do the worst jobs around the mill, and usually were forced to pay kickbacks to their ethnic "bosses" as well).

But he concluded it was the fault of the mill owners and not the economic system .

Besides, a job was a job, and he wouldn't be staying long.

In 1935, representatives of the unemployed and the Relief Camp Workers Union organizing the On to Ottawa Trek came to the mill looking for support. They received none from Steuart.

A year later, an industrial accident cost him his job. Part of a finger was cut off in a saw and partly for safety reasons and partly as a reprimand for carelessness, the company demoted him. Steuart would not accept the demotion so he quit to return to Saskatchewan.

His experiences in British Columbia had obvious impacts on him, but in many ways they were contradictory. "It gave me a suspicion of governments, unions, businesses, anything which was involved in letting that [the Depression] happen." But later, when the war started and suddenly the government had money to spend the country out of the Depression, he began to see the potential for using the wealth and power of government to help people and influence events.

Those conclusions were years away when the twenty-year-old left Vancouver in 1936. He was simply looking for a job and the road led back to Prince Albert, where his father and brothers were planning to open a grocery store. He became involved in the family retail business, and except for several years as a navigator on Royal Canadian Air Force wartime flights overseas, he worked in the business and watched it expand into an electric shop and then a hardware store. The merchant business provided him an economic base and a stake in the future of the small northern Saskatchewan city. In a way, it would also be his springboard into local politics.

Steuart was a political slow starter. He claimed no political affiliations during the traumas of the thirties, and although his parents were Liberals, the party held little attraction for him. He cast his first vote in the 1940 general election when he joined his parents in voting for Conservative Ray Manville, a family friend, against Liberal Prime Minister William Lyon Mackenzie King (a successful Liberal parachute candidate in the mid-twenties who represented the riding until a personal defeat in 1945).

The war began to politicize Steuart. He was a strong supporter of the war effort and conscription and felt betrayed by Mackenzie King when he appeared to be soft on conscription. Yet his first public political speech came during the war and it was in favor of that same Liberal government. The night before the general election in 1945, Canadian airmen gathered in a mess in Ireland were giving impromptu political speeches. Most were anti-Liberal, so partly in fun and partly to balance the rhetoric, Steuart climbed onto a table to deliver a speech entitled: "Mackenzie King, the Soldier's Friend." It was less than popular. "They kept tipping the table and throwing beer at me," he recalls.

When the war ended, Steuart returned to Prince Albert to resume his place in the family business. In 1946, he married Eunice Ray and appeared to be settling into life as a prospering businessman.

But the political climate had changed and it was to lead Steuart into the fray. In 1944, the young Baptist preacher T. C. Douglas had led the leftist Co-operative Commonwealth Federation into power in Saskatchewan with promises of a stronger government role in the economy and creation of more state-supported social programs.

Steuart didn't know yet what he was for, but he did know what he was against. "I came back to Saskatchewan and found they had elected a socialist government," he said. "I was very suspicious of anybody who claimed to have a masterplan. So I got into politics."

It wasn't quite as simple as that, of course. Steuart still didn't have a party affiliation and it was several years before he decided the Liberals would be the best vehicle to use in the fight against the statism he was growing to hate. It was, he said, a matter of chance that he chose the Liberals. "If the Conservatives had been more active, I might have been drawn to them. I really backed into the Liberal Party. It wasn't until later that I began to take an interest in what they believed in."

By 1949, he was working for the provincial Liberal party in the provincial election and becoming involved in local party affairs. However, it was in the municipal arena that he scored his first political successes.

In 1951, he decided to run for the city council in Prince Albert to counter a slate being offered by the CCF. He was elected on his first attempt, and during the next decade he won consistent re-election to council, served two terms as Prince Albert's mayor and one term as president of the Saskatchewan Urban Municipalities Association.

They were years of active growth for Prince Albert, and Steuart was usually at the centre of the work. He campaigned tirelessly for improved services and more industry for the city. He waged highly publicized and ultimately successful campaigns for airport improvements, a new bridge in the city, and more industry for the area. He took on the Saskatchewan Power Corporation in a battle of words over electrical rates and service in the city, and during his years as mayor, he held down tax increases and clashed publicly with the school board when it did not. The once virtually bankrupt city completed its first successful bond sale in forty years.

Steuart was a highly visible and highly popular civic politican, and that gave him a vehicle with which to promote himself for bigger things. Throughout the fifties, he became more deeply involved in Liberal party affairs, and by 1959 he was a power to be reckoned with. That was the year in which he was instrumental in deposing then provincial leader A. H. McDonald and convincing former CCF firebrand Ross Thatcher to become party leader. Steuart was elected party president, and although he was an unsuccessful Liberal candidate in the 1960 provincial election, he found a home in the Legislature after a by-election win in 1962.

As a key Liberal organizer and a moving figure behind the party's obvious revival, Steuart's election on November 14, 1962, brought Liberal reaction from across the country. Although he had to share the spotlight with Quebec Premier Jean Lesage, whose Liberal government won re-election for a second term the same day, Steuart's victory created a stir. Federal Liberal leader Lester Pearson telegraphed "warmest congratulations;" Senator John Connolly wrote that he had heard the news broadcast in Paris while attending a NATO meeting; Walter Gordon wrote from Ottawa: "You will be a tremendous help to Ross Thatcher and the Liberal cause not only in Saskatchewan but everywhere in Canada."

On February 14, 1963, Steuart was sworn in as the newest member of the Saskatchewan Legislature. At forty-seven years of age, he had another platform from which to wage his holy war against "socialism."

During the next two years, Steuart played a key role in promoting Liberalism in the province. Alone or with Thatcher as the straight man to his rousing humor, Steuart travelled thousands of miles, preaching the gospel of free enterprise, personal initiative, and the need to get rid of "the heavy hand of socialism."

When the medicare controversy broke out, he was quick to join forces with the anti-CCF groups. He played a key role in the Prince Albert Keep Our Doctors committee and preached the evils of state medicine. By the time of the 1964 provincial election, Steuart and his supporters were sure enough of themselves that they ran a newspaper ad proclaiming: "Elect Steuart, the man already assured a key position in this government."

The voters of both Prince Albert and Saskatchewan took the cue. Steuart was re-elected with a slim seventy-eight-vote lead and the Liberals ousted the CCF after twenty years of rule.

True to the ad, Steuart occupied key positions in the Thatcher government. He took on the heavy portfolios of health, natural resources, and finance at times when those jobs were in the forefront of implementing Thatcher government policies. After June 3, 1965, he was also deputy premier.

His years as a government leader were controversial. Detractors said his role in bringing Parsons and Whittemore into the province's forestry industry marked him as a man who would sell the province to the highest bidder; defenders said it proved he could attract economic activity if given the chance. His tenure as finance minister came at a time when the provincial economy was on a downturn, wheat prices were low, population was declining, and voter discontent with the government was growing. He contributed to the chaos with his 1968 budget raising taxes, and it led to further economic stagnation. Although the budget was largely Thatcher's creation, Steuart was blamed for it and was widely regarded as Thatcher's economic hatchet man.

Critics of the Liberal government record saw Steuart as one of the two main symbols of the repression and conservatism of the regime. Liberal true-believers saw him as a prophet, unafraid to tell people they should expect no more out of the system than they put in.

Inside the party, hidden from the glare of publicity he so often dominated, Steuart played the vital role of mediator — the person who could keep warring factions of the party cemented together, who could appear to be on both sides of a party question at once. When Liberal MLAs were unable to get Premier Thatcher's attention or felt left out by his blunt, one-man approach to government, they would take their problems to Steuart and he would raise them with the premier during their daily late-afternoon talks. A former senior party official described Steuart's go-between role this way: "If a MLA wanted something done, he would go to Steuart to see the best way of getting it past Thatcher."

Steuart played a similarly conciliatory role in the battles between the federal and provincial Liberal parties. Even when tensions were highest between Thatcher and federal Liberals, Steuart was the main federal contact in the Saskatchewan government.

Publicly, however, he played the political game of "fed bashing" as well as anyone. In his 1968 budget speech, for instance, he spent some time attacking the federal government for not devising economic policies which recognized regional differences. The following year at the federal-provincial first ministers' conference in Ottawa, he was one of the leaders of the successful provincial campaign to lay many of the country's problems at the feet of federal economic policies.

By the time he assumed the party leadership, Steuart's image had been defined by his public past. His record revealed attitudes and perceptions which helped propel him into the leader's office, but which also made the reawakened left wing of the party uncomfortable with the delegates' choice. They would have a bearing on how well he could be sold to Saskatchewan voters during the next four years.

Primarily, he was anti-NDP with a hatred honed during the heyday of Saskatchewan's politics of polarization. To despise the NDP was reason enough to be a Liberal.

He was pro-business to the point of being vulnerable to attack as a sell-out politician. He believed future prosperity lay in industrialization, and if the government had to be an active agent offering concessions to attract the necessary capital, that was the price of progress. Steuart's stance on that issue was consistent throughout his political career at both municipal and provincial levels. In August 1952, while a Prince Albert alderman, Steuart cautioned city residents against becoming too vocal against a bad smell emanating from the Prince Albert Refineries plant. "We are more than interested in getting just as many industries as possible to come into Prince Albert and if we [council] make a quick decision and order the refinery closed down because of a smell, it might keep other industries out," he said. Nineteen years later, he included in his 1971 budget speech in the Legislature an attack on economic nationalists who would thwart the Liberal dream of financing industrialization with foreign capital: "They are a strange combination of NDP socialists, communist professors and a few Canadian businessmen from eastern Canada. They all have one thing in common. They are frightened by outside competition, they are living off the backs of the Canadian people and are afraid of losing their cozy set-up." Some critics saw this as a Liberal policy because the party depended on foreign-owned businesses for much of its funding. More realistically, it was the gut response of a group of free enterprisers who felt private initiative from anywhere was better than government involvement.

Supplementing his pro-business bias was a deep-rooted distrust of unions. During his successful 1962 by-election campaign, brochures said Steuart's three years in B.C. during the thirties helped "instill in him a deep understanding and sympathy of the problems and needs of labor." Yet he considered the labor unions enemies, useful mainly as whipping boys when he talked about the "labor bosses" who would run the province if the NDP won election. Steuart supported in cabinet the antilabor Bill 2 which gave the government the right to prohibit strikes in government-designated "essential services."

Next to the NDP, his biggest enemy was bureaucracy. He consistently blamed civil servants in both Ottawa and Regina for many of the problems he saw with government. When the Liberals assumed office in 1964 and Steuart met his senior health department staff for the first time, he described it as walking into an "enemy camp." Years later, as finance minister in charge of trimming the "fat" out of government, he delighted in catching the civil servants trying to have unnecessary expenditures approved. He had departmental budget bureau staff infiltrate various departments to report on the validity of annual budget requests. Once he forced a delegation of civil servants from the education department to drive him from his Legislature office to their offices to show him typewriters they said should be replaced. Steuart found the existing typewriters in good working order and turned the request down.

A comment on cost-shared programs at the 1969 federal-provincial first ministers' conference illustrates his contempt for bureaucrats and what he saw as their self-serving empire building: "I am sure that if the bureaucrats were given a magic wand they could wave to solve the problems of cost-shared programs, they would hide the wand or break it."

Steuart's political record showed a curious mix of conservative self-righteousness and humanism. His speeches on personal initiative and welfare abuse made it clear he had risen from humble origins and others should be able to as well. Yet the record of the Thatcher government, and Steuart's personal record, on concern for helping native people get a piece of the economic action was good. He was compassionate with those he felt were left out through no fault of their own. He was unforgiving in the face of those he considered statists or freeloaders.

He was almost the total politican, and as a result his private and family life suffered. In the Steuart family, the rearing of the two children was left mainly to his wife, Eunice. As politics played a greater role in his life (beginning in the early 1950s), his private life decreased. Associations with Prince Albert community groups such as the Elks and the Royal Canadian Legion were gradually and quietly dropped in favor of evenings with other politicians or evenings alone. "I soon had few close friends who were not in politics," he says. "The trouble was that if we went out with non-political friends, they bugged you, felt they had the right to tell you off and monopolize your time. Politicians tend to stay with each other. They don't bug each other."

By the time he reached the Legislature and then government, Steuart practiced politics almost non-stop. Once a year, he and Eunice would vacation together alone, but in Saskatchewan, they had little time together. His private escapes became reading biographies and mysteries or golfing.

Politics changed Steuart's life and his lifestyle. Friends in Prince Albert had been fellow merchants, long-time acquaintances, or other locals. In politics, he was dealing with a more exotic group of people — businessmen used to big deals and pressure — and Steuart began to feel more comfortable with them. While he considered several political colleagues, including Thatcher, as part of his inner circle of friends, several high-profile businessmen the government dealt with also became intimates. Peter Jack, Saskatchewan boss of the Potash Company of America, and Jack Turvey, president of Regina's Interprovincial Pipe and Steel Company, were sometime advisors and friends. New York capitalist Karl Landegger of Parsons and Whittemore was the most important of these new-style friends. Steuart was fascinated by his toughness in negotiations, his "19th Century views about capitalism" and his progressive views about the need for some government regulation in the public interest and high death taxes to prevent transfer of wealth between generations. "He broadened my horizons about a lot of things," Steuart said. He and Landegger developed a private friendship in some ways more important to Steuart than their official dealings.

He looked upon his associations with these "high rollers" as a perk of the job, a privilege he would not have had as a small-time Prince Albert businessman. They reinforced Steuart's views about the creativity and energy of the private sector. It impressed him that he was able to associate with them on equal terms. They were people he could learn from. "That was one of the side benefits of politics," he said later. "I would not have known people like this. I found them fascinating."

In his public life, Steuart combined a fierce partisanship with a genuine sense of humor and an eye for publicity. His skills of hustings oratory were second to none in the province, and he could turn his natural and finely tuned sense of humor on himself to win sympathy or commitment. He could also turn it on the party to make Liberals laugh at themselves and see the problems in their party. (When he wanted to chide provincial party members for being too interested in the attraction of power at the federal level, he would tell the story of losing part of his little finger in a freak accident in a Liberal election committee room during a campaign. The phone rang, he would say, and when he reached to answer it, eight others in the room grabbed for it as well in case it was a call announcing an Ottawa appointment. The finger was lost in the ensuing melee.)

When he took over as leader, Steuart's major task was to motivate the party, to pull it out of the defeat mentality. His philosophy was to lead by example, and over the years he had paid his dues as a good, loyal party man. During the 1950s and 1960s, he worked long hours to mend fences, keeping the party alive and motivated. He knew his place in the hierarchy in those days and was prepared to follow orders from those above him.[1] He was, in the words of Colin Thatcher, son of the former premier and not a Steuart fan, "perhaps the best number two man a number one man could have. I often heard my father say that."

In the next four years, Steuart's challenge was to throw off that image of a number two man to become a leader in his own right. To do that, he would have to cash in some of the IOUs from his dues-paying days. It was the only way to survive in a party accustomed to strong, dominant leaders.

[1] One of the best illustrations of his attitude toward authority in the party came the morning after the 1964 Liberal election win. Although Thatcher and Steuart had been "close friends," Thatcher kept Steuart waiting in the outer office for some time before he would admit him to talk about the future. Steuart said he was hurt but accepted it as "an indication of the new relationship. He was premier."

Chapter Five

AN ATTEMPT AT REORGANIZATION

One of the legacies of Jimmy Gardiner and Ross Thatcher was the perception that the Saskatchewan Liberal party was a powerful political machine capable of working its territory in search of support. As far as the new leadership of the party was concerned, that perception was largely myth — a throwback to the days when the Liberals ruled the province through patronage and consensus politics. That, however, was close to three decades and twenty years of CCF government out of date. While Thatcher had revitalized the flagging party structure and scored impressive gains with such indicators as memberships and rallies, the new leaders felt the organizational strength of the party in 1972 was shallow. In the 1971 election, it had failed the ultimate test of a political party organization — getting the vote out. If the NDP was to be beaten, the Liberals would have to build a better organization.

Dave Steuart spent the final few weeks of 1971 in the Caribbean, resting from the leadership race and planning for the future. When he returned, he showed associates the outline of a plan for rebuilding the party. It met immediate resistance from President Garry Wilson, who considered it too grandiose, too idealistic, and too expensive. In part, the debate was over which of the two would have control over the party apparatus. In the end, a compromise was worked out which was less grandiose, and although it was still expensive, Steuart took responsibility for raising the funds to pay for the upkeep of the structure. With some refinements, it became the official game plan, approved by the executive in September.

A major premise of the outline was that Liberals had to look beyond policy errors to explain the recent defeat. They had to look at themselves and what they had done or had not done for the cause. "A major reason for our defeat," it said, "was that we simply didn't have a good enough organization to identify our vote and get it out to the polls."

The analysis quickly became conventional wisdom for a large section of the party. In hindsight, it was an easy answer: although party memberships were high and enthusiasm appeared to be there during the election, large portions of the party had become apathetic or complacent. Members felt they had little control over the party or the government and worked only as hard as they had to. The party concentrated on the visible activities such as membership drives, socials, and public meetings as indications that it was healthy. It failed to motivate people to involve themselves in the organization, or even to vote. "Our election campaign organizations (and especially the identification and dragging out of our vote), were simply not up to par," said the organization paper distributed to key party members.

The proposed answer was easy to enunciate and difficult to make work. The party should switch its emphasis from the top to the bottom, said the proposal. Strong organizations should be constructed in each of the approximately 3,000 polls in the province, and these poll organizations would be the basic and most important unit in the new Liberal party.

To convince people to take the generally thankless and time-consuming job of running a poll organization year-round, the leadership proposed that the status of the poll captain be raised. Close contact would be maintained between the poll captain and head office, and both power and inspiration would flow up the organizational chart instead of in the traditional down direction.

Once poll captains were picked, they would form committees of prominent Liberals, and these people would be responsible for yearly canvasses, attracting new members and keeping the party visible in their areas. These activities would be supplemented by formal membership drives, fund-raising, political meetings, and youth work. Riding executives would be responsible for their areas, regional directors would be responsible for coordinating their larger areas, and the provincial office would be the overall coordinator. Party leaders and the caucus would show up when they were needed, as well as carry their share of the load in Regina.

The reorganization proposal set the sights of the party high. "If we can only make the poll captain feel needed and important, then maybe, just maybe, we can whip up a good active organization in 80 per cent of the polls before 1975," it said.

The proposal was hardly new. "It was just basic political organizing, You'll find it anywhere," said party Executive Director Dave Sheard. But it did represent a departure from the recent history of the Saskatchewan Liberals.

The proposal to make local organization the key unit in the party and to make the various levels of the executive important parts of the overall plan was a break with what the party had become under a series of strong leaders — a vehicle for their ideas and election.

The Liberal party did not have a tradition of diffuse power. It elected strong leaders and then waited for them to produce a victory. In the first forty years of its life, the party was usually governing and its leaders practiced a form of group government, co-opting pressure group leaders into the party and then counting on them to provide the voter support. The tactic worked well in government, but it was not suited to Opposition. During the CCF years, the Liberals maintained their position as the alternative to the government only because no other right-wing challenger with mass political appeal emerged.

Thatcher changed the lethargic existence the Liberals had been leading. He introduced membership drives for the first time, attracted strong people to the party executive, and began to appeal directly to voters with an energetic program of campaigning.

Once elected to government, however, the emphasis began to change. Thatcher dominated the party, the executive, and the caucus. He demanded and received loyalty. His ideas triumphed, and gradually the party became largely a vehicle to promote Ross Thatcher's ideas and to re-elect him to implement his dreams.

In 1977, a former senior party official wrote, in an analysis of declining Liberal fortunes prepared for internal party use, that after the 1967 election Thatcher assumed "almost complete domination over his cabinet, caucus and party in matters of policy and organization. The last traces of party input as the government's listening post began to disappear."

The effect, critics argue, was a stifling of party membership enthusiasm (although power or the prospect of power attracts its own followers, waiting for the gravy train or simply anxious to be identified with a winning effort). It led to the half-hearted effort Steuart and the party elders complained about in their proposal for reorganization. It made the idea of organizational decentralization a radical one.

Soon after the 1971 convention, the executive also made it clear it expected to play a major role in the new order. An executive meeting was held early in 1972, and Steuart told them he not only would let them play a greater role, he expected it.

The reorganization plan appeared to receive enthusiastic and wide-spread acceptance in the party (although concrete steps to implement the poll-level organization did not begin until the next year). It was a sign the leadership had learned from past mistakes. The promises of change made at the convention were being fulfilled.

In fact, 1972 was a good year for the party. Membership interest was at a reassuring level, constituency organizing began throughout the province under the direction of the executive director Dave Sheard, and at the fall convention, enthusiasm was high. Prime Minister Pierre Trudeau, recently humbled by the voters who returned a minority Liberal government in the October 30 federal election, chose that convention to make his first post-election public appearance. Delegates were buoyant and party leaders felt they were on the right track.

It was also a year of two significant organizational successes for the party — winning the Athabasca by-election and re-establishing links with the party's out-of-province financial backers.

Finding the money was the easier of the two. The Liberals traditionally had little trouble tapping businessmen and antisocialists for donations. The pitch was made that as the site of the earliest and most aggressive social democratic government in Canada, Saskatchewan was the front line of defence against socialism. It rarely failed to bring in funds, and Thatcher's $935,000 kitty was proof of past successes.[1] But what would the attitude of moneymen be to the new leader and the fact the Liberals were no longer in power? The reorganization plan would require additional funds, and Steuart was determined to pay for organizing from current revenues, rather than dipping into the bankroll.[2] During the winter of 1972, the new leader led a delegation east to find the answer. Dinner meetings were arranged at prestigious clubs in Montreal and Toronto, and business leaders from those cities turned out to hear the new Saskatchewan Liberal leader.

Steuart was in top form, blasting the "socialists," calling the Saskatchewan NDP the first wave, and warning the corporate leaders if they did not help fund the fight in Saskatchewan, they might soon be fighting it on their own doorsteps. His basic pitch was that workers employed by the companies represented at the meeting were supporting the NDP through union check-offs. If they wanted to counter that and work for a political system they supported, the businessmen should fund the Saskatchewan Liberal party more frequently than once every four years at election time. The job of fighting socialism is fulltime, he said, and the Liberals needed money regularly to keep the battle going.

The morning after the speeches, members of the group, including party executive officers, visited the businessmen in their offices to try to turn the nighttime enthusiasm into daytime dollar commitments. The trip was a success. Some companies had adopted a policy of no political donations, but many others agreed to ante up. Later in the year, similar trips to meet oil executives in Calgary and grain industry officials in Winnipeg were just as successful. "I would say those trips outside the province brought in $100,000 a year," says one party official.

Funding, it appeared, would not be a problem — at least until threatened legislation to control political financing became a reality.

---

[1]Shortly after the new leadership took control, they decided the party should do something more creative with the money than bank it. Under pressure from President Wilson, they purchased a building and a lot of land along a main commercial street in Regina for about $70,000. It not only gave the party a central headquarters from which to run the party and elections, but it also gave the party a lucrative investment. Within six years, the value of the property had more than doubled.

[2]Information about annual party budgets is not made public, but a party source said that in that era it was more than $200,000 per year.

Although it was being threatened then, two more years would pass before it became law.

The Athabasca by-election was a more public event, an uncertainty which turned into a morale-boosting victory. On the face of it, the Liberals had everything to lose and nothing to gain from the September 27 vote. Former Municipal Affairs Minister Allan Guy won the seat in 1971 by a twelve-vote margin. The result was challenged in court, and on February 14, 1972, a Court of Queen's Bench judge controverted the election, ruling there were sufficient doubts about the outcome to declare it null and void. Although the party had held the huge northern seat during the sixties, by-election prospects had not looked good. There would be a strong voter tendency to support the NDP with the sure knowledge they would be electing a government member who would work to see NDP election promises of greater northern self-government implemented, Liberal planners thought.

The party threw itself totally into the by-election campaign. Organizers, MLAs, the party leader, and as many workers as could be found flooded the riding as summer turned to fall. On election night, Guy won re-election by a slim thirty votes, despite a concentrated NDP effort to win the seat. The Liberals were buoyant. They felt the victory showed voters the NDP was not invincible and that the Liberals were far from being a dead force in the province.

During the next two years, some of that optimism continued. Party leaders continued to put faith in the new, decentralized structure by assuming local leaders would work out problems as they became apparent. In December 1973, the party electoral machine was tested again and scored a victory. The traditionally Liberal Regina Lakeview seat became vacant when the sitting MLA died, and despite a strong NDP campaign, the Liberals retained the seat in a by-election and increased their lead. The victor was a lawyer, Ted Malone, an old-wealth establishment Liberal. The win gave the party a chance to celebrate and to point out that since the general election, Liberals had won three of four by-elections.[3]

Throughout 1974 and 1975, reports flowing into Regina head office were positive as organizers established a party presence, encouraged local organizations, and looked for candidates across the province. Steuart was successful in attracting young, aggressive, and appealing candidates in many areas. Nominating conventions in many ridings were producing huge crowds. Private polls conducted for the party showed the NDP weak in some areas of the province with issues such as government ownership of farm land through the Land Bank Commission and the catch-all concern of "big government" touching a voter nerve. "The polls indicated we were

---

[3]The Liberals had won by-elections in Morse, where Jack Wiebe replaced Ross Thatcher, Athabasca, and Regina Lakeview. The lone NDP victory came when lawyer Kim Thorson retained the Estevan seat won by the NDP in the 1971 general election. It had been vacated by a death.

succeeding in creating issues," says a senior party official. The bad news was that the polls also showed Steuart was not as popular as Blakeney and that there were areas of the province where the Liberals were not catching on. "We knew the truth. The leader and the party weren't all that popular in some ways," Executive Director Sheard said later.[4]

That was the other side of Liberal fortunes during 1973 and 1974. Despite the optimism and genuine signs of organizational progress, there were also clear signs that the Liberal revival plan had some flaws.

By 1973, the previous year's momentum was slowing down. The provincial economy was becoming stronger, many initiatives of the NDP government were proving popular, and Allan Blakeney remained better liked and respected than Dave Steuart. Liberal organizers were also finding it hard to translate the enthusiasm of 1972 into the hard work required in 1973. Efforts to establish a strong organizational base across the province were meeting with only limited success, and it was proving difficult to find poll captains willing to do the work required. Mid-term apathy was setting in.

In 1974, the danger signals increased despite official optimism. Organizational goals were not being met. Flaws in the system were becoming apparent, and the party seemed unable to correct them. In some cases, the problems were not even recognized until much later, when it was too late.

The most obvious problem area was at the local level, which was to have been the key to the Liberal revival. There were continued difficulties finding hard-working poll captains, and solid organizations were being put into place in fewer than half the ridings, according to several key party planners. In others, work was less than adequate or virtually non-existent. "It's really difficult to get poll organizations going until election time," Sheard said later.

A debate was also developing within the party about organizational strategy — should the party aim at electing Liberals in all available ridings or concentrate its power and hopes in a few strong or potentially strong areas? It was a debate which was not to be resolved until late in the 1975 campaign although the lines were drawn as early as 1973. One group felt Liberals in all ridings should be given an equal chance to win, with as much party support as possible. Another felt the only way the Liberals had a chance of forming a government was to concentrate firepower, at the risk of alienating some key people in the ridings left off the priority list.

---

[4]The polls were conducted by Decision Making Information Canada of Edmonton. They began questioning population samples in September 1973 and continued with increasing frequency until late in the 1975 election campaign. The polls proved both a blessing and a curse. They helped identify issues and NDP weaknesses, but these were often misinterpreted by Liberal officials to represent party strengths. In many cases, the discontented voters were not happy with the Liberals either, but that did not register on the polls.

Other problems were beginning to surface as well. Despite Steuart's attempts to put his own stamp on the party organization, it was basically unchanged in key personnel and local methods from the days of Ross Thatcher's revival. At the same time, one of his innovations — the attempt to decentralize authority — was manifesting some flaws. It meant MLAs were responsible for organizing in their own seats, and indications were appearing by 1974 that in some ridings held by Liberals, organizations were weak. MLAs Cy MacDonald and Allan Guy had been hired as organizers, and this led to charges they spent more time in their own ridings than in the total area they were supposed to organize.

There was also concern that in some ridings unsuitable candidates were being chosen and Steuart was refusing to interfere to affect the outcome of the constituency choice. "He was not the dictatorial type guy," Sheard said later. "It was one of his strengths but sometimes, it also turned out badly."

Critical party officials say the constituencies of Estevan and Rosthern were two examples where a firmer hand from Steuart might have averted candidate problems. In the southeastern Saskatchewan riding of Estevan, a former MLA and twice-defeated candidate Ian MacDougall won the nomination. Many swing voters or strongly anti-NDP voters were unhappy with the choice and eventually switched their vote to the Progressive Conservatives. The influence of that flowed into two surrounding ridings, and the southeast became a disaster for the Liberals. In hindsight, Steuart conceded he should have tried to stop the MacDougall nomination. After two consecutive defeats, he had a reputation as a loser. "He was the wrong candidate," Steuart said later. In some eyes, Allan Guy was also the wrong candidate in Rosthern, a heavily Mennonite constituency north of Saskatoon. Guy was a divorced man and a longtime MLA for a northern riding who parachuted into Rosthern thinking it would be a safe seat because it had long voted Liberal. He found both the parachute landing and the divorce worked against him, and the Liberals eventually lost the seat.

In both cases, the seats appeared to be there to be won by the Liberals, but a combination of poor candidate choice and either a head-office refusal to intervene or inability to see the developing problem led to defeat.

On another front, the Liberal leadership was running into criticism from the opposite end of the spectrum. Some members of the executive felt the resolve to decentralize power away from the top was not going far enough. Donna Welke of Regina, provincial party vice-president at the time, says many on the executive felt they were being excluded from decision making as they had been under Thatcher. Despite a commitment from Steuart after the leadership convention to encourage and support greater strength and independence in the executive, she said he was uncertain about how far to carry that and it caused some internal tension. Executive members often felt they were being excluded from the real decision making and that the power was still being hoarded by Steuart and a small group of colleagues, including the president Wilson and the executive director Sheard. "At executive meetings, I often felt we were dealing with just the tip of the iceberg," Welke said later.

Discontent and disillusionment were the result.

One indication of the internal tensions and growing concern about evident problems was the rhetoric Steuart adopted during this period. Despite earlier criticism of Thatcher for falling back on membership numbers and social gatherings to illustrate party strength, Steuart began to do the same thing in the year before the expected election. He used every occasion possible to point out large nomination turnouts, the growing membership list (over 30,000 members), and the number of Liberal events being organized in the ridings. It was, he argued, an indication of membership enthusiasm. The discredited symbols of the past were being resurrected and presented as truths of the present.

While party officials fought to overcome organizational flaws and some disarray, they were also faced with two more vexing problems — an unexpected downturn in party financial fortunes and the longstanding Saskatchewan dilemma of how to deal with federal Liberals.

Chapter Six

FINANCES AND FEDERAL LIBERALS

One of Dave Steuart's first acts as Saskatchewan Liberal leader was to attempt reconciliation with the governing federal Liberals. Shortly after winning the leadership convention, Steuart met privately with Otto Lang to suggest a truce. "I told him the feud was over," Steuart said later. "There's no question that the guerilla warfare that went on hurt all the Liberals and gave the NDP a field day."

Guerilla warfare? Truce? These seem like strange words to use in describing relations between sections of the same political party, but in the case of federal and Saskatchewan Liberals, they were appropriate.

The history of relations between the two groups is as much a story of tension and feuding as it is of cooperation and shared battles. Although they shared some of the same political goals and a largely interchangeable membership base, the two factions often found themselves at odds over ideology, finances, tactics, or personalities.

It was an uneasy, often private struggle which had been going on for decades. It broke into the open during the sixties in the bitter public disputes between Ross Thatcher and various federal Liberal leaders. By the dying days of the Thatcher government, relations between the two levels of the party had almost completely broken down.

Steuart wanted to change that, although during the sixties he had been a willing and often leading participant in the Ottawa bashing. As leader, he proposed an end to the tension and the introduction of a new era of cooperation in which both sections would stake out their areas of interest and defend them, but they would also aid each other's cause when a fight was on against a common enemy.

Steuart's intentions may have been good, but it was not to be. The federal-provincial split had primarily been a struggle for power to control Liberal fortunes in the province. By 1972, the balance was shifting to the federal Liberals, and they were not about to negotiate an end to the struggle just when they were winning. By that time, the divisions were too entrenched and the players too stubborn to compromise. The humiliations of the Thatcher years' snubs would be repaid.

By 1974, this was becoming obvious to the provincial Liberal organization. Federal-provincial relations were undoubtedly better, but it was often at the expense of the provincial party.

Superficially, the basis of the dispute was a disagreement over tactics and political posturing. As a tactic of governing, federal Liberals often co-opted the policies of the CCF-NDP and looked to that small federal group as potential allies in the face of attacks from the real opposition — the Progressive Conservatives. The result has been a federal party which has promoted income redistribution, expansion of the welfare state, and other policies which conservative Saskatchewan Liberals considered socialism. Provincially, the Liberal enemy was the CCF, and unlike the federal party, Saskatchewan Liberals looked to PC voters as potential allies against the CCF-NDP. Federal policies and cooperation with the NDP made provincial Liberals uneasy. Provincial Liberal attempts to woo PC voters made federal Liberals uneasy. There was little room for electoral coopera-tion.

The reasons for the dispute were more fundamental than political tactics, however. At issue was who would control the provincial party apparatus and finances. The winner received not only prestige and some limited power, but also authority over the steady flow of patronage which comes from controlling the federal government.

Constitutionally, there is no dispute. The party constitution provides only for a Saskatchewan Liberal Association. It is the sole party representative in the province, and federal activities should be just a part of it. In practice, that was not always the case. In the early days of the province when strong Liberal premiers were in power, the provincial party was supreme and the federal Liberals looked to strong provincial organizations for their electoral base. However, during the heyday of Jimmy Gardiner in Ottawa, the provincial party was run largely from the federal level. Although he held no formal position in the provincial structure, Gardiner was powerful enough to commit provincial Liberal funds without receiving prior provincial approval.

Ross Thatcher changed that. He took over the provincial party a year after Jimmy Gardiner had lost his seat in Parliament, and he insisted on directing all Liberal affairs in the province. Federal Liberal activity in Saskatchewan would be part of his jurisdiction. The first challenge to that edict came at the 1960 provincial party convention when University of Saskatchewan law professor Otto Lang championed a proposal that the federal wing be given some official recognition and some executive seats. Thatcher opposed the idea and won the day.

Federal Liberals were displeased but there was little they could do. Out of government and without a strong Saskatchewan leader, they had to bide their time. A breakthrough came in 1962 when Thatcher, after a personality and policy dispute with federal leader Lester Pearson, refused to throw full provincial support behind the federal Liberal cause in an election campaign. Pearson appointed Lang as Saskatchewan campaign chairman, and Lang quickly assembled a group of thirteen lawyers to organize the federal effort. (Based in Regina and Saskatoon and each responsible for one of the province's ridings, these new recruits were quickly dubbed the Regina "Silver Seven" and the Saskatoon "Silver Six" by detractors.) The election squad was chosen more because of their loyalty to Lang than for their political skills, and it showed. Not a single Liberal was elected in Saskatchewan. The next year they were back again with the same result, but in those disasters the seeds of a separate federal organization had been sown. Lang had shown Thatcher the provincial apparatus was not needed for federal campaigns.

Thatcher was outraged, and when he formed the government in 1964, the provincial party was the Liberal power base. The premier demanded, and received, control of all party activities. Lang's influence receded, but he still remained the focal point for intellectuals or others in the party either dissatisfied with Thatcher's style of government or more naturally interested in federal affairs. Many were lawyers who had studied under Lang at the University of Saskatchewan. They were bright, loyal, and ambitious.

Otto Lang was a peculiar choice to be the focal point for what was essentially an underground political group. He had yet to prove himself as a politician or a capable infighter. His ventures into politics had been largely unsuccessful, and he was both an uncomfortable campaigner and an uninspiring speaker. His image was that of a quiet, arrogant intellectual. Yet he also carried an air of success. He had been raised in the Humboldt area east of Saskatoon, became a brilliant student and a Rhodes scholar, and was appointed professor of law and then dean of law at the University of Saskatchewan before he was thirty. He was a recognized constitutional expert and a strong believer in some classical liberal philosophies on the role of rationalism, individual initiative, and freedom of action. He was married to Adrian Merchant, a member of a prominent Saskatoon Liberal family, and the couple eventually had seven children.

Lang held a theoretical, scholarly view of political systems, constitutional arrangements, and the need for rationality in politics. But he also held some emotional views, strongly influenced by his Roman Catholicism, against abortion and capital punishment. Supporters, who often became intense and defensive disciples, found him brilliant, hard-working, principled, and compassionate. Critics found him arrogant, stubborn, and reactionary.

Throughout Thatcher's first term, Lang maintained a low political profile but kept alive his contacts with both federal Liberals and potential future allies across the province.

In 1968, when Pierre Trudeau won the Liberal leadership, Lang decided to give in to pressure that he become a candidate. Trudeau was also a rationalist and constitutional lawyer who would apply the forces of logic to the nation's problems, and Lang had found a political soulmate. He won the Saskatoon-Humboldt nomination for the June 1968 election and squeezed past his election opponents to end more than a decade of Conservative hold on Saskatoon. His victory margin was 555 votes. Lang quickly gave up his position as dean of law, took a leave of absence from the university, and flew to Ottawa and a cabinet post in the new government. He also became the chief federal Liberal spokesman for Saskatchewan and the focal point of the provincial party divisions. The separate federal organization, outside provincial control, was reborn.

Despite the unity prescribed in the party constitution, two distinct organizations continued to develop during the next three years, and Saskatchewan Liberals often had to choose between them. Thatcher was suspicious of anyone considered a Lang loyalist, and a small group of federally-oriented Liberals who felt out of place in the provincial party began meeting Saturday mornings to discuss policies and priorities they did not feel they could introduce into Thatcher's party.

"I think Ross was sometimes suspicious of anyone loyal to me," Lang said later, although he tries to play down that period of division. Another party official recalls: "You could not ride both horses. The easiest way to cut someone's throat in the provincial party was to tell Thatcher he was a Lang man."

After 1968, the small elite of federal Liberals grouped around Lang began to develop some clear roles: its members reviewed patronage rolls, including federal appointments, grants, and other federal largesse for the province; they were primarily responsible for selling federal policies and programs in the province; and they were responsible for federal election planning in the province. In effect, a separate organization grew to ensure Lang that his policies would be sold and his power preserved, no matter what the strength or inclination of the provincial party.

Steuart saw the danger of this, and as leader, he set out to try to end the split. He arranged for regular consultation, ended public sniping, and committed substantial provincial resources to helping the federal Liberals in the 1972 and 1974 campaigns (when Liberal strength went from one seat to three).[1]

Ironically, however, it was under Steuart that the federal-provincial split was formalized. At an executive meeting at North Battleford in the summer of 1973, the executive approved a Steuart motion that the federal affairs committee organized by Lang be formally recognized. The proposal first came from President Garry Wilson when he found himself without any

---

[1]Provincial Liberal help in the 1972 election was not entirely altruistic. Before the campaign, senior officials met Lang in Saskatoon to pledge provincial help if Lang would let the party have some say in federal patronage and appointments in the province. Provincial officials say Lang agreed, but the agreement broke down shortly after the election.

say over federal affairs in the province. He thought by including federal planners in the provincial organization, the provincial party would be able to assert some control over them, or at least have an influence. Steuart later rationalized that the move was a good one because the federal group existed anyway and a formal recognition of that would let the provincial party turn its attention back to strictly Saskatchewan issues.

However the real effect was to legitimize and expand the power of Lang and his federal followers in the province. Although theoretically accountable to the provincial executive, the federal affairs committee owed its true allegiance to Lang and it quickly drew up its own constitution making it clear the provincial party had no control over it. With its own budget, a structure in Saskatoon, and direct links to the governing Liberals in Ottawa, the federal affairs committee became a major Liberal power centre in Saskatchewan.

Finances were the next major battlefield, and again the provincial party was the loser. Fund-raising had long been one of the party's strong points, and early in Steuart's tenure as leader, money seemed the least of the party's worries. Thatcher's legacy had allowed the purchase of a valuable piece of Regina property and although the reorganization plan was a costly one (staff was increased and expensive organizers were sent around the province), Steuart quickly proved he could raise enough money to pay expenses out of current revenue.

In 1974, the provincial government ended that with election expenses legislation requiring political parties to limit campaign spending and to account for it. More damaging for the Liberals, who strongly opposed the legislation, was a requirement that the donors of more than $100 had to be identified. When Liberal fund-raisers went out that year, the effect was obvious. Many traditional corporate backers wanted to avoid public identification with any political party so they refused to donate.[2] The party had to look increasingly to small Saskatchewan contributors, and the $100-a-plate dinner quickly became a major source of funds. Party officials also began to prepare to dip into the Thatcher kitty as the election approached.

The federal Liberals offered a solution to provincial money woes, but at a price. Through a recently-approved federal election financing law, provincial Liberals could have access to new reserves of money, but they would have to be distributed by the federal party.

The operation of the funding scheme was simple and attractive. For each $100 contributed to a federal party, the donor would receive a $75

---

[2]There were, of course, ways to work around the new law. Toronto capitalist Michael Sifton, owner of Saskatchewan's two largest daily newspapers and, at the time, Regina's largest radio and television stations, used his media holding company Armadale Limited to contribute to both Liberals and Conservatives without being publicly identified at the time. Cheques for $100 were sent to individual candidates, and contributions totalled several thousand dollars during the election campaign.

rebate at income tax time from the federal government. The national parties could then distribute part of these funds back to provincial affiliates, as long as the money sent to provinces was being used for federal political work. Although the legislation was clear on that point, the line between federal and provincial political work is thin enough that the rebate scheme was obviously an important new source of funds for the provincial Liberals. Practically, it also presented a problem for provincial fund-raisers. Without a comparable rebate scheme for donations to provincial parties, contributors would be more willing to donate to the federal party. The provincial party could be left looking to the federal party more and more for a cut of its funds. Provincial officials felt they could not ignore the benefits of the scheme because money was needed to replace diminishing corporate donations.

However, there were several disquieting aspects of the deal from a provincial Liberal point of view. Traditionally, the party had been the fund-raiser for both federal and provincial activities in the province, and it was a bitter blow to some to have the federal side now providing more of the funding. More practically, there were concerns about the added powers administration of the scheme would give to the federal Liberals and the Lang organization. Controlling the money is a powerful weapon in politics, and provincial officials saw several ways the fund could be used by the federal affairs committee to enhance its position — there could be arbitrary decisions on what portion should go back to provincial organizations, and decisions on how the money should be used could be heavily weighted toward federal, rather than provincial, affairs.

Saskatchewan Liberals quickly focused their efforts on arranging a formula which would govern distribution of the money between federal and provincial organizations and which would take any discretion over its distribution or use out of the hands of the federal Liberals who might use it as a bargaining lever.

The federal legislation was approved in 1973, and although it was not to take effect until after the next election, the federal Liberal party immediately created a fund to handle money raised. Federal-provincial Liberal talks on distribution also began immediately, and federal officials proposed a complex formula which would have provided money for the operation of federal constituency organizations, an election fund, and day-to-day operational expenses of provincial organizations in proportion to their federal efforts. The proposal was unacceptable to several provincial Liberal organizations, including Saskatchewan, in part because they felt it was too vague and did not spell out which "day-to-day" expenses provincial parties might claim.

After months of bargaining, a formula splitting the money fifty/fifty during off-election years and seventy-five/twenty-five during election years (with the majority going to the party level fighting the election) was approved on an interim basis until after the next provincial Saskatchewan election. It later became standard.

Despite the paper agreement, however, provincial Liberals were still suspicious of the power the fund gave Lang and his followers. Steuart continued raising as much independent provincial money as possible. When the scheme began to operate in July 1974, provincial fears were soon confirmed. A small group of Lang confidants was established outside the formal structure of the federal affairs committee to administer use of the money. The party's official agent, lawyer John Stack, was in charge of distributing it. There were provincial complaints that this shadowy, Saskatoon-based group was under the control of no one but Lang and that despite the formula, it still had the power to decide when the provincial share would be distributed. This created planning problems for the provincial party.[3]

There is no doubt the federal scheme was an effective fund-raiser, and party officials say about $300,000 was raised in Saskatchewan through the rebate plan during the first six months of 1975. However it made the provincial party increasingly dependent on the federal party for funds. The attraction of donating twenty-five-cent dollars to the federal party made it almost impossible for the provincial party to raise its own money and gain some independence from the fund. It was a vicious circle which created tensions and damaged pride. Increasingly, the provincial party was being undermined organizationally and enslaved financially by the federal wing.

Provincial Liberals also had to bear the brunt of public disapproval of many federal Liberal policies, although they had little control over either the policies or the way they were presented in Saskatchewan by federal spokesmen.

As the 1975 provincial election approached, Liberal efforts at organizational reform during the previous four years deserved mixed reviews. On the surface, an organizational base appeared to have been established across the province, including an attractive array of candidates, more than enough money, and some enthusiasm based on the presumption of NDP vulnerability. But beneath the surface were some weak spots, including an inadequate system of political intelligence and some weak organizational links. The decades-old federal-provincial feud was also still simmering, and on several fronts the provincial wing was losing the fight.

---

[3]True to his goal of healing divisions within the party, Steuart did not play a tough role in this developing dispute, although he was a key negotiator. In later interviews, he denied having trouble getting the provincial allocation from the fund, despite contrary statements from other officials.

Chapter Seven

IN SEARCH OF A POLICY

If there was one area in which Dave Steuart and the new leadership wanted the Saskatchewan Liberal party to have a new look, it was policy development. Immediately following the 1971 convention, the party launched a voyage toward a 1975 election-campaign platform which was to take it into largely uncharted waters of internal democracy, membership activity, and the catch phrase, "grassroots involvement." It was the most ambitious and controversial part of the effort to change the face of the party, based on explicit instructions from delegates that they wanted a policy review started after the leadership convention. Specific instructions on the formation of committees and the need for a review were contained in a resolution passed at the leadership convention. For the first time in years, and possibly ever, party leadership was to offer the membership a key role in determining what the Liberal party stood for and where it was going.

The last major attempt to do this had come in 1955 when leader A. H. McDonald mailed questionnaires to members, asking their policy preferences for consideration by provincial council members. The effort failed to have significant impact on later policy positions of the party. In the Thatcher years, defenders of his leadership style said he was in tune with the membership mood, but it is more properly interpreted that the membership was willing to accept Thatcher's policy ideas.

The new effort was to be different, and members were to be offered a formal vehicle to make their views known. In the end, judgments about the three-year effort are ambiguous; the perceptions of its real impact were unclear. The most obvious result was that it failed to propel the party to victory. For some in the party, that meant simply it was a noble experiment which had fallen short. To others, it meant the effort was a failure, a charade, a disillusioning experience.

Above all, it taught Liberals about themselves and the type of political person the provincial party attracted. Their strong point was knowing what they did not like, rather than what they liked. Their long-range program goals were ill-defined while their immediate political aims were crystal clear — reduce the power of government and bureaucracy, and let the inherent logic of the marketplace work things out. For those left behind by these economic forces, society should provide a safety net of protection. The extent of policy initiative should be to weave that net.

The development of policy was a problem for some Liberals because it implied that, in government, the party would play an activist role. "The policy formulation was a difficult process, as we found out," Executive Director Sheard said later. "If you don't believe in growing government, you probably have a hard time coming up with imaginative policy about things you do once you are the government."

However, in 1972 these lessons had still not been taught to Dave Steuart. He had just emerged from a leadership convention at which he felt one of the strong membership messages was that they wanted more say in determining party policy. After years of being told by the leaders what they stood for, the members wanted to start talking back. Steuart had also been deeply impressed by the impact of the 1971 New Democratic Party election platform, New Deal for People. It had been skillfully written to offer an alternative to the stand-pat stance of the ruling Liberals and to convince voters that an active government could lead them into better times. The program was articulately presented by the NDP, and voters stampeded onto the bandwagon. In that process there was a lesson for the politician Steuart, and he was determined to apply it to the Liberal party.

It was a lesson he wanted all party members to understand. In an April 1972 speech to young Liberals in Prince Albert, Steuart drove home the point that the party must have a positive policy alternative. "We must build a positive approach so we can present a positive platform and philosophy so the people can look at the record of the NDP and at what we have to offer and make a clear choice," he said. "If we do the job right, we will not only win but we will deserve to win."

In the reorganization document produced by Steuart in early 1972 and later ratified by the party executive as the plan which would lead the Liberals back into power, the goal was clearly and simply stated: "The party should provide the membership with a meaningful opportunity to participate in the process of government."

Steuart had decided one of the downfalls of the Liberal government the year before was that policy had been created at the top and it was out of touch with the mood of the electorate. The mechanics proposed in the reorganization plan to correct that flaw were straightforward: in each constituency, a policy committee should be formed to encourage and collect ideas from the membership and to pass them on to the elected MLAs and party leaders. These committees would meet with local interest groups to get ideas for party policy, hold public metings, and then apply their new-found voter intelligence to the issues of the day. Through direct meetings with caucus members or by passing ideas to an official in Steuart's

Regina office, the party leadership would always know what people in the province were thinking.

The plan also called for a provincial organization of committees to provide the basis for the 1975 election platform. Committees with constituency representation would be formed, hold hearings across the province, study policy alternatives, and in the end, play a key role in developing the election platform.

The idea was enthusiastically adopted by the party, and in 1972 the policy committees were established to deal with a number of policy areas — agriculture, the environment, health and welfare, business development, mineral resources, education, and intergovernmental relations. Hardworking party members from throughout the province were chosen to chair the various committees, and they were all to be under the direction of a committee of the provincial executive chaired by Gerry Fraser of Saskatoon, a party director and former aide to Ross Thatcher. The committees' work was to be monitored by Steuart's executive assistant Jim Roche in Regina. His role was to offer assistance and to make sure the committee work was receiving the attention of caucus. The ideal, said the party reorganization plan, was that the "ordinary membership holder should have a mechanism whereby any good policy idea that he has will ultimately end up being expressed on the floor of the Legislature through one of our MLAs."

While it hardly seems like a revolutionary idea in political organization, it did represent a substantial change for the Liberals, who had traditionally been long on direction from the top and short on membership participation. During the Liberal years of power, leaders rarely consulted members of the party about policy. A clear indication comes from the fact that between 1931 and 1946 the party did not hold a general convention.[1] After the party's 1944 defeat by a policy-oriented CCF, Liberals struggled for years to counter both the organization and policy strength of the CCF, which pioneered techniques of party democracy in the province. While CCF leaders were important catalysts in policy formulation, constituencies and local members were given considerable input through resolutions and debate at annual conventions. A. H. MacDonald, during his five years of Liberal leadership, tried to copy CCF techniques by offering members a direct say in policy through the mails but the idea had little impact. During the Thatcher years, general conventions were held most years, and there was at least the appearance of membership input, but the conventions were little more than forums for approving the actions and policies of the leader. They were not noted for their wide-ranging debates. In making his proposal, Steuart hoped to introduce some of the NDP ideas of membership involvement into the Liberal party.

For a party with so little tradition in membership policy involvement, the idea caught on quickly. Fraser recalls that in the early months of the experiment leading up to the 1972 annual fall convention, committees were

---

[1] Smith, *Prairie Liberalism*, 253.

set up in many constituencies, ideas were flowing in from members and the process appeared to be thriving. Enthusiasm was high. "From Day One, there was always the understanding that when it came to writing a platform, the campaign committee would decide what would be emphasized," says Fraser. That prospect gave the groups their inspiration. However, from the beginning there were also problems of inexperience and a lack of direction. "For us to get the rank and file Liberals involved in policy development was quite foreign to them and we really lacked a lot of the expertise to make the thing work," he said.

Others took a less charitable view of the problem. John Embury, later party treasurer and president, and in 1972 the chairman of the business policy committee, said party members were not able to respond to the challenge. "A lot of their resolutions were crap," he said. "They'd vote for anything."

The problem which developed early in many of the committees was a lack of focus for the discussions. The party had renounced many of the policies of the previous Liberal regime and they were searching for a new direction. However, because of the large numbers involved and the fact that many had never been seriously involved in policy formulation before, they were drifting. Party leaders hoped the chairmen of the policy committees would provide the focus. Most of the chairmen looked to the leaders, particularly Steuart.

"I think the idea could have worked if there had been a group of policy people to lead," Regina MLA Ted Malone said later. "That didn't happen." Moose Jaw MLA Don Macdonald added: "I don't think you can get that many people meaningfully involved. Steuart didn't give it the needed focus."

There were two basic reasons for Steuart's deliberately low-key approach. He wanted the policy committee process to reflect real party views and not the views of the leaders. Any attempt by him to "focus" the discussions would have appeared to be an attempt to fall back on the old way of forcing policy from the top. A more fundamental reason was the political outlook of Steuart and many of the advisors around him who learned the process under Ross Thatcher. They were doers, not thinkers. They believed governments are defeated because of mistakes, rather than opposition parties elected because of attractive policies. "Dave is like myself," a former cabinet colleague Cy MacDonald said of Steuart. "I'm not a policy person. I'm more political . . . that was a weakness in Dave. He's not a policy man."

Still, while the flaws in the system quickly became apparent to some and the old-line faction of the party was dubious about the wisdom of opening the policy doors to the common crowd, the overwhelming party reaction during the first year was enthusiasm.

Among the key enthusiasts were former supporters of George Leith — the so-called 171 Club members who voted for Leith on the first ballot of the leadership convention. Steuart was able to keep many of them involved by promising them he had read the convention message that the party had to open its eyes to new ideas and escape the dogmatic days of the sixties. They included Barb McNiven, who became a party official and key organizer; Donna Welke, a policy committee member and later vice-president; and other key workers, usually young, who enthusiastically joined the search for policy as a way to revitalize the party and make it fit more readily with their views.

The 171 Club title was really a misnomer. The group would informally congregate at conventions and some were friends, but they never formed an official lobby group within the party, as the name suggests. The influence they had came largely from the efforts of individual members.

Steuart's method of dealing with this potential inner-party opposition was to try to give them a role and make them feel comfortable. Within two years, the separate identity of the group had largely disappeared. "They were an important part of the policy process," Steuart said later. "I included them. I never felt threatened by them. But some people in the party were not happy that I accommodated them."

In late 1972, the party members got their first chance to inspect the work of the committees at the annual convention in Regina. The committees presented resolutions to the convention and asked for delegate votes to offer some direction on the issues. The plan was that after the convention the committees would discard ideas rejected by delegates and develop more fully ideas given majority approval.

Delegates provided a snapshot of their convictions on scores of topics. Ninety-four percent voted to oppose the provincial government's land bank program for farm land and to support a program of government guarantees on loans taken out to allow farmers to buy their own land. Seventy-nine percent voted to replace welfare with work-incentive programs in small towns. Fifty-six percent decided draft dodgers should not be allowed to settle in Canada because they take jobs away from Canadians. Delegates also strongly supported (69 percent) a proposal that one Liberal be appointed in each constituency to seek policy ideas from such non-party groups as municipal councils, school boards, labor, and student groups.

During 1973, the committees were supposed to continue their work and submit more resolutions to the annual fall convention, reflecting both more work on resolutions approved the year before and proposals for positions on issues which had become prominent during the previous year. The result was a further refinement in policy ideas. Issues were debated at the convention and delegates voted later, by mail. Ninety-six percent of those who voted were still opposed to the land bank and in favor of a program which would encourage land purchases rather than renting from the government. Large majorities voted to give more power to municipal and local governments in a number of areas. Eighty-nine percent voted to get provincial governments out of controlling any aspect of cable television. Fifty-one percent voted to widen the net of medicare to cover the cost of dental, optical, and prescription drug costs, and 84 percent voted to provide more funds to rural schools for upgrading the quality of education.

In total, delegates in 1973 sent scores more resolutions to the committees. A mood was beginning to emerge in some areas — delegates were remaining hard-line in areas like welfare, private enterprise, and opposition to NDP moves which they felt centralized power in Regina. But they were also willing to agree to sometimes-costly programs which appeared to be attractive vote-getters in tune with the voter mood of getting more from government. Some in the party saw this as a form of socialism creeping quietly into the party, and ideological tensions sometimes surfaced.

At the 1973 convention workshop on health and welfare, committee members were promoting a resolution calling on a Liberal government to encourage, and if necessary fund, a system of daycare centres. Right wing MLA and former cabinet minister Dave Boldt rose to suggest that woman's place is in the home, raising the family, and any party support for daycare would simply be another move toward letting women out of their rightful place. Party officials quickly dissociated themselves from Boldt's statements (much to the delight of the media which played up the Boldt statements), but he did represent a body of opinion within the party. Colin Thatcher, son of the former premier and a member of the party's right wing, complained later that "no one would walk into the room and ask those people where the money was going to come from."

Steuart, on the other hand, appeared to be concerned that the party was being too conservative at the convention. At one point, when delegates showed they were strongly against existing welfare programs but did not have a very clear idea of what could replace them, he told them: "Let's not be deluded that social reform is socialism. Don't think the NDP are the only people who can bring in reform." Later, he told delegates: "Stop thinking every time we're spending a nickel we're socialists."

During 1973, the first real concern that the policy committee idea was not working began to surface in the party. In May, Steuart sent a letter to constituents in which he said he was disappointed with the response the committees were getting. As leader, he said, he had promised to "open the party to all those who were interested in contributing their ideas to our policies and platform. I have kept that promise. Unfortunately, the response has not been as good as I had hoped."

By the end of the year, policy committee chairmen were living with the reality of that disappointment as they began to run into organizational problems.

Original plans to have the committees tour and hold public hearings were scrapped because of the cost. Some of the initial enthusiasm had died down, and it was becoming more difficult to get committee members to meetings or party members to offer ideas or to take an interest in the process.

This trend was to become more pronounced in 1974. The job of the committees that year was to reduce the volume of material to a few major, well-researched issues which could be debated at the fall convention and then form the basis of the election platform. Instead, many of the committees slowed down that year and did little refining. Debate at the 1974 convention was as wide-ranging as it had been during the previous two conventions, and when the talking was over, party officials were left with a large number of resolutions approved and little coherent philosophy around which to build a campaign platform. After several meetings with policy committee chairmen, senior party officials decided a group so large and diverse would not produce a concise and salable platform before the expected summer election. As late as April 14, councillors, caucus, and candidates were still arguing over what to include. A committee of three — Roche, Sheard, and Wilson — was formed to write a platform to be taken to caucus.

As the document was being drafted, policy committee chairmen felt themselves excluded from the process. It left some of them bitter and disillusioned at a time when their energy and commitment were needed in the party. "I was disappointed that the policy committees didn't have a strong say in the final policy product," said coordinating committee chairman Fraser. Health and welfare committee chairman Jim Serne of Saskatoon was less diplomatic. He said he was bitter that the policy committees had lost control of their product. "It was an honest attempt to get grassroots support. We worked hard. But when the dust cleared, I felt it was a waste of time."

Not all those involved in the committees felt they had been wronged, though, and party officials who decided to take the final policy writing out of the hands of the committees felt they were justified. "Somebody had to write the platform and the election was coming," said a senior party official. "The committees had done their work. But they were going nowhere in getting it boiled down."

The booklet which emerged from the process during the winter of 1975 was a strangely disoriented document. Steuart called it a blueprint for "a new direction for the government of Saskatchewan, one based on our belief in the inherent greatness of Saskatchewan's citizens and in the great potential of our provincial resources which, if properly utilized, could make our people among the most self-reliant in the nation." Others saw it another way. It was a mixture of traditional free enterprise belief in the private sector and government give-aways aimed at an increasingly demanding electorate. It offered the prospect of a lean, spendthrift government while promising new programs which provincial government economists, working at public expense at the direction of the NDP government, estimated would cost taxpayers hundreds of millions of dollars. (Steuart estimated the cost at $150 million to $200 million.) It lacked the philosophical purity required to attract the right wing or the welfare state commitment needed to convince skeptics on the other end of the spectrum that the Liberals really were on a "new direction." Above all, it was a document of political expediency which tried to tap the voter mood.

The major emphases of the policy paper were agriculture and resource development. Party leaders argued that if these two major resources of the province were fully developed, the economy would boom and increased taxes would be used to pay for all the expensive social programs the voters apparently wanted and the party seemed willing to give them.

The agriculture program was an attractive one for the Liberals. It proposed government aid to farmers wanting to buy land and a gradual phasing out of the government land bank program of farmers leasing land from the province. It suggested changes in the government's foreign ownership of land restrictions and proposed that product marketing boards only be established with the ballot consent of affected producers. In the touchy area of transportation and grain hauling, the party supported retention of the Crowsnest Pass statutory freight rate on grain movement and suggested its benefits be extended to livestock and finished agricultural products.

In resource development, the party proposed to undo what it saw as NDP mistakes by taking steps to improve the business climate and to attract investment. It promised to abolish the controversial provincial oil tax legislation and to replace it with "fair taxation rates" after negotiations with the oil companies. It proposed to reduce government intervention in resource development and to encourage more activity and exploration by the private sector.

In other areas, the party proposed: welfare reform to help those able to find work and to end "waste and mismanagement" in the program; a minimum monthly income guarantee for senior citizens of $350 for singles and $500 for couples; more money and autonomy for local governments; more funds and an upgraded standard of education in rural schools; changes in the health care system, including more grants to special care homes and ambulance service throughout the province; incentives to small business to expand or upgrade operations; more money for rural communities to improve services; immediate cablevision for the province; and changes in labor laws to protect union members from retaliation if they publicly criticized their union.

On the surface, it appeared to be a comprehensive, if somewhat disjointed, statement of what the Liberal party believed. Steuart described it as "the most comprehensive and sensible policy statement ever made by a political party in Saskatchewan." Public statements emphasized it as a true reflection of the mood of party members after more than three years of probing and policy development.

In some cases, notably agriculture, that was true. The agriculture committee, under the chairmanship of University of Saskatchewan professor Doug Knott, was the most effective link in the party's policy efforts. It managed to tap the main trends of party thinking on the issues while being open-minded enough to consider the points of view of non-Liberal industry, pressure, and producer groups. One indication of Knott's open-minded approach came in the first year when he and the committee asked the 1972 party convention if the left-wing National Farmers Union should be allowed to represent farmers if it received the majority of farm support. The idea was supported by a surprisingly large 22 percent of the delegates. The idea was then dropped by the committee, but it indicated to the party that all avenues of thought had been canvassed. When the policy platform was written, most of the committee's main recommendations were accepted and included.

Other committees did not fare as well. In many policy areas, the platform was simply a reflection of what the small core at the top of the party felt would sell. If committee recommendations did not fit that view, they were ignored.

One of the hardest hit was the health and welfare policy committee. Members worked hard to develop a very liberal program, ranging from state-supported daycare and an expansion of medicare to a proposal that the federal Liberals be pressured to settle native land claims, pass laws against child abuse, and develop a negative income tax program. The final election platform ignored all these areas and it drew some bitter feelings from committee members.

There were similar exprinces in other committees. Proposals for more money to establish kindergartens, construction of a pulp mill in northwestern Saskatchewan, and a suggestion that there be controls on foreign investment in the province were ignored by the platform writers, either because they felt them impractical, too costly, or too unpopular.

At the same time, platform planks appeared which committee officials said had not come from them, including the commitment to bring cablevision to the province immediately.

The issue of women's rights provides a good example of the tensions which the policy development process created in the party as both the old and the new schools tried to have their ideas reflected in the final product.

Attempts by several high-profile party women to have a strong women's rights plank in the platform were rebuffed, despite a strong pitch by Steuart to involve women more in the party. Delegates first responded in 1973 by approving a resolution calling for a marital property law which would recognize the concept of equal partnership in marriage and equal division of marital property in the event of a divorce. The vote in favor was 74 percent. However, when the platform was published, it contained just three specific proposals for women: a commitment that a Liberal government would treat women in the civil service more equally; a commitment to make benefits for women under the government automobile insurance scheme more generous; and a commitment to support and use "the tremendous resources of women in volunteer organizations."

Party Vice-President Donna Welke of Regina said later she found the commitment to volunteerism inadequate and infuriating. But earlier efforts by herself and other top-level women in the party to have "a strong policy regarding women's rights" included in party policy were unsuccessful. She said she raised the issue at an August 1974 provincial executive meeting and the reaction was anything but encouraging: "One gentleman stated that the women candidates could look after this area and one potential woman candidate replied she was tired of a group of 'women libbers' screaming about women's rights. After the applause ceased, the subject was dismissed."

In spite of the criticisms from some party members and the obvious flaws of the final document, the party and Steuart had accomplished something by producing it. His leadership campaign had been based in large part on a commitment to open the party up to more control by the membership. For the first time in memory, party members had been asked to play an active role in the policy formulation process, and many had responded. It had been an undisciplined exercise and in the end broke down when the final shape of the policy had to be designed by the party leadership in a move reminiscent of the old days. But Steuart and his group were pleased that anything had emerged from the process. They felt the attempt at offering members a say would help rid the party of the dictatorial image it had acquired in the public mind.

There was some disappointment that more party members did not become actively involved, however, and it led leaders like Steuart to some unpleasant conclusions about the make-up of the Liberal party. Many of the party leaders had been convinced all the "grassroots" needed to grow was a little encouragement, but in the end much of the committee work had been done by a small minority of party membership, and interest seemed to die as the process wore on.

Steuart concluded that in Opposition it is hard to get people to do anything but react. He blamed party membership for the failure to become involved and concluded most party members were willing to let the NDP define the issues they were supposed to react to. "The people who are attracted to the Liberal Party are not the people who are attracted to the idea of policy making," he said. It was an opinion voiced often by party leaders who felt let down by party members.

Not everyone accepted that judgment. Some turned it back on the leadership, arguing the policy-creating process would have been more successful if the leaders had been more interested and played a stronger role.

"That policy attempt was made because the people were clamoring for it," Executive Director Sheard said later. "It was really just a bother for many of us. The top guys really didn't believe that policy would win the election."

The health committee's chairman Jim Serne blamed Steuart for much of the failure. "I'm sure he thought it was all window dressing. This was for public consumption and not really to involve the membership. I think it was a ploy on his part to show the people of Saskatchewan that the party was open."

Gerry Fraser, chairman of the executive coordinating committee for policy development, saw it as a failure on both sides. "That's why we have leaders and followers," he said. "People want to be led . . . when you talk about grassroots involvement, you are really talking about a small number of people who want to get involved and do the work."

The attempt to change the policy-making system within the Liberal party succeeded in making some changes and producing a policy. But in a party not used to the experience, it also left a lot of people looking for someone else to blame.

Chapter Eight

THE SASKATCHEWAN POLITICAL WARS, 1972-75

While many of the energies of the Liberal party were being directed at internal, less visible areas such as policy formulation and organizing, there was also a public, political battle to be fought. Voters and party members alike had to be shown that there was an active, aggressive, and competent Liberal team in the province, despite the defeat of 1971. From a Liberal point of view, the province had to be shown that the new NDP regime was not infallible and that the Opposition was not a spent force.

The leaders of this Liberal campaign would be Dave Steuart and the fourteen-member caucus that survived the election. The object, according to the party's four-year game plan, was to have the caucus become more responsive to party sentiment while gaining public credibility as a strong, united alternative. "Basically, caucus needs to be built up as a strong team that can form the next government," said the game-plan manifesto.

In part, the success or failure of that goal would depend on the issues which arose during the next four years and how the caucus handled them. The other part of the formula was the quality, commitment, and competence of the caucus members themselves. In Saskatchewan's politically-sensitive electorate, the performance, consistency, and depth of the MLAs would be closely watched and harshly judged. Steuart contributed to the pressure on individual caucus members by trying to impose a more egalitarian style of leadership on them — he expected them to be informed, active, and visible during the next four years. Dr. Don Macdonald of Moose Jaw, a freshman member of the caucus, said Steuart deliberately tried not to dominate caucus discussions so other MLAs could have an impact. "When he came to caucus with an issue, he wasn't willing to lead," recalled Macdonald. "He was just one of the group. It was an attempt to be democratic, perhaps too democratic. At times, he wasn't strong enough."

Many in caucus saw this approach by Steuart as a reaction to Ross

Thatcher's brand of strong, uncompromising leadership. Some saw it as a sign of weakness in the new leader, while others thought of it as his way of challenging caucus members to play a greater role. In many ways, it was a challenge which the caucus was ill-equipped to meet. Being in Opposition was an unexpected shock to most of them. Out of fifteen, only Steuart, Allan Guy (Athabasca), and Dave Boldt (Rosthern) had experience as Opposition MLAs. Once the shock of losing government had sunk in, several appeared anxious mainly to survive the next four years so they could get out of politics. The first-time members like Macdonald, Ken MacLeod (Regina Albert Park), and Gary Lane (Lumsden) had campaigned expecting to be elected as government MLAs, and it took some time to readjust their mind set.

The caucus had no lack of experience. Six of its members had cabinet experience and eleven had previous Legislature experience.[1] However, the public and the party did not always see that experience translated into effective caucus action. Some, like caucus member Tom Weatherald, thought the record was a good one. "I believe caucus was effective. We had nine or ten very good members out of fifteen. The others were either retiring or disinterested." Others saw it differently, or at least put a different interpretation on the facts. Steuart complained later that the caucus was often unenthusiastic, and despite his efforts to lead by spirited example, he found it hard to motivate the others. Caucus member Dr. Macdonald characterized most of the caucus as "weak" and he concluded it was filled with members who preferred to take easy shots at the government rather than to research their issues and make positive suggestions. Ted Malone, who entered caucus in late 1973 after winning a Regina Lakeview by-election, found it generally a closed group with little apparent interest in his ideas or his attempt at initiative. With a few exceptions, including Steuart, Malone said he found the attitude to be: "You won. So what?"

Political and legislative experience is usually considered an important contribution to a struggling party, but in the case of the caucus Steuart inherited, some observers thought it may have been overdone. Stirling King, then editor of the *Saskatoon Star-Phoenix* and a former Thatcher aide, saw the caucus as "a lot of rusty old members who hadn't grown with the years. They were still campaigning 1958 style."

Inevitably, it was a group with strengths and weaknesses. As the term in Opposition wore on, more and more of the workload fell to the handful willing and able to do it and maintain a high profile. Steuart increasingly carried the weight of showing public leadership and trying to convince the

---

[1] The former cabinet ministers were: Steuart, who had been finance minister and deputy premier; Cy MacDonald, welfare minister; Allan Guy, municipal affairs and head of the Indian and Metis department; Dave Boldt, highways and welfare; Cliff McIsaac, education; and Gordon Grant, variously industry, highways, and health.

party and the public that he led a spirited and competent caucus. On many days, its performance made a liar out of the leader.[2]

As the new party leader, there was nothing Steuart could do about the strengths or weaknesses of the caucus willed to him by the voters. He could only try to understand them and exploit their strengths while playing down the weaknesses. His own position was different. The voters' judgment of his performance would play a large part in the success or failure of the party in the next election. The task would require full exploitation of his known talents for hard work and humor, but much more. He would have to grow from being a Liberal's Liberal into a politician who could appeal to a far broader voter base. He would have to throw off the well-entrenched image as a number two man and become known as a leader on his own merit. He would have to keep steady and effective pressure on the programs and policies of an obviously popular government.

All this would prove to be a tall order which would have to be dealt with on three levels — doing battle with the NDP on a day-to-day political basis; proving he was capable of rising above politics occasionally to become a spokesman for the province against outside interests; and developing a public relationship with the ever-present federal Liberals which would end the divisive bickering of the past, while avoiding the politically damaging image of becoming too subservient to federal Liberal interests.

Considering his history as an organizer and political scrapper, Steuart was obviously best suited for his role as an NDP critic, and he threw himself into the job with gusto. Although he missed few opportunities on various speakers' platforms during the next three years to criticize the government, the major battlefield was the Legislature, where he was recognized as a master of rhetoric and the art of point-scoring. During the next three years, the government gave him ample targets to fire at as the NDP moved quickly in a number of areas to implement their election promises. While many of the policies met real needs and were likely to be popular with many voters, Steuart saw them as part of the socialist master plan to take over the province and to centralize control over almost all areas of life in the hands of the hated bureaucracy.[3]

The 1972 Legislature session became a showcase for NDP initiatives.

---

[2] One indication of the lack of enthusiasm many had for their Opposition role is the high attrition rate between elections. By 1975, six caucus members were quitting or had left. Gordon Grant, George Loken, Dave Boldt, and Don Macdonald did not seek re-election. Dr. Cliff McIsaac ran successfully for the House of Commons in the July 1974 federal election. Ken MacLeod accepted an appointment to the Court of Queen's Bench early in 1975.

[3] Steuart and the Saskatchewan right wing use the term "socialism" to describe almost anything which runs counter to their own philosophy. It bears little relationship to the economic definition of socialism. They use it to describe anyone who favors increased government intervention in the economy, or public ownership of anything which could be operated privately.

The government proposed creation of four new departments, appointment of an ombudsman, and establishment of a system of land banking which would see the government buy land from retiring farmers and then lease it to young farmers. Steuart and the Liberals put on a spirited display of negativism and obstruction. They opposed creation of a consumer affairs department because they thought it would give government too much power to interfere with small business. They opposed creation of an ombudsman's office because Saskatchewan was not big enough to justify the expense (although Liberal MLA Ken McLeod voted with the government). The Liberals complained about high unemployment and government increases in welfare spending. And they objected to creation of a single administration for northern Saskatchewan through creation of the Department of Northern Saskatchewan.

However the Liberals' most damning rhetoric and energetic fight was saved for the government land bank proposal. In their eyes, it was state farming, and in a province heavily populated with first and second generation East Europeans, Steuart blatantly equated the land bank proposal with state farming in communist countries. Liberals fought it in the Legislature, took their arguments to meetings throughout the province, and appeared before public hearings called on the issue.

The major argument was the wording of the legislation which said that after five years the government "may" sell the land to the renter. The Liberals said if the government planned to sell the land, the legislation would have read "will," and the government's refusal to make the change was proof to them that it planned to buy and never sell huge pieces of Saskatchewan farmland. At times in his attacks, Steuart slipped into Cold War slogans. "We support a sensible land bank program where you can either buy or rent the land," he said in one Legislature speech, "but not one that is aimed at nationalizing . . . yes nationalizing the land. What's the difference between a socialist and a communist?" The land bank issue was one of the Liberal success stories. They kept hammering at it throughout the three years, and by election time it had become one of their most effective issues.

During 1972, Steuart also began scoring points on another issue the Liberals would use effectively during the next three years — the relationship of the NDP to the business community. He considered many NDP policies antibusiness, and each time a new regulation appeared to control business or a new bill was presented which raised taxes or increased regulation, Steuart would charge the government with conducting a war on business which would end up strangling the provincial economy. At the end of his first year as leader, Steuart sounded the warning: "Someone in Mr. Blakeney's ivory tower had better realize that if they want to solve the problems of unemployment, population losses and the deaths of our small towns, they had better start making a serious effort to attract industry to Saskatchewan."

By then, Liberals felt they had reason to be pleased with their performance and their new leader. The small Opposition caucus had certainly shown it was up to the fight, and they felt that in several areas the government had been put on the defensive. Public reaction to the party, particularly on the land bank issue, had been good. However, the year's performance also showed up a developing flaw in the structure — while Steuart was telling the party they had to develop a new, positive look, the public performance of the caucus was a throwback to the socialist-baiting days of the sixties. The theme of most speeches was to attack, rather than to propose alternatives. Part of the reason was that the party was just beginning to develop policies to counter government programs. But a major reason was Steuart's own style of politics, enhanced by several other caucus members who had learned the rules under Thatcher. The game was to attack, the tone was negative, and the motto was "Governments aren't elected. They're defeated."

The new year began with more of the same. The Legislature session began in late January, and the Throne Speech proposed creation of a Crown oil company, more power for the government over the timber industry through Saskatchewan Forest Products (a Crown corporation), and amendments to the Natural Products Marketing Act governing establishment of agricultural marketing boards. Steuart immediately saw it as another step in the master plan: "The Throne Speech, for the first time, lays before the public the resource development policies of the NDP government and for the first time since they were elected, Premier Blakeney is showing his true colors." The Liberal leader said debate would "divide the men from the boys on the subject of socialism versus free enterprise."

Steuart quickly found support in the *Regina Leader-Post*, a newspaper always anxious to find an ally in its fight against "doctrinaire socialism" and the reality of Saskatchewan history for twenty-one of the previous twenty-eight years. "The thing to watch as the session gets underway is not the usual interplay of legislative tactics between the government and the Opposition but rather the former's parliamentary technique to put across step-by-step progression into the socialist version of paradise," wrote the *Leader-Post* editorialist.

Not surprisingly, the "parliamentary technique" used was the government majority in the Legislature, with the will of 55 percent of the electorate behind it. But despite the minority role and sure defeat, the Liberals carried on with motions, private member's bills, and debate to oppose and delay while trying to mobilize public opinion.

Looking at the land bank and the proposed changes to the marketing board legislation which did not guarantee a producer vote before a board was established, Steuart expanded the attack to describe what he saw as the NDP move to take over agriculture — first buy the land, then control how producers can market their product, then restrict foreign ownership of land and pass succession duty legislation to hurt the transfer of farms between generations. Added to the argument were controversial government moves to impose, without a producer vote, a hog marketing board and the purchase for more than $10 million of less than half-interest in a Saskatoon meat-packing plant Intercontinental Packers. It was all, Steuart argued, a carefully laid plan to restrict personal freedom and to take over the industry.

On top of that, the Intercontinental Packers purchase appeared to show that the government leaders were bad businessmen. Steuart produced figures to argue the entire plant was not worth $10.2 million, and although the government denied all the charges, the Liberals persisted. They appeared to be scoring some points.

An issue which appeared ready-made for the Steuart master plan theory came in late 1973 when the government introduced legislation to increase substantially levies on the oil industry and to control oil company income from the province. The Liberals immediately attacked it as another front in the war on business, and they offered a spirited opposition in the Legislature before the bill was approved.

The oil issue turned out to be less than a bonanza for the Liberals, however. It came at a time of soaring international oil prices, and Saskatchewan was simply following the Alberta lead in trying to capture some of the "windfall profits." Federal oil policies were unpopular at the time, and Steuart had a hard time separating himself from them. Provincial Liberals could not attack Saskatchewan policy without appearing to defend the oil companies — not a popular position in a province which had long felt itself exploited by such eastern or foreign based companies. The NDP made the most of provincial Liberal ties to federal oil policies and labelled Steuart an apologist for big business because of his attacks. In response, the Liberals had to find a policy of their own, and the result was not very inspiring. Steuart's alternative was to argue for high taxes and government power to regulate prices through a marketing board which would set a lower price for current oil and a higher price for new, more expensive oil. There would be more consulting with the oil companies, but no government power to break lease agreements or to nationalize reserves.

Steuart called it a "middle of the road" policy but it appeared to contribute little to the debate. Early in 1974, the Liberal position became even more muddled when Premier Blakeney failed at a federal-provincial conference to win his demand for an oil price increase to nine dollars a barrel. Overnight, Steuart changed his tactic from one of criticizing Blakeney for being greedy and trying to gouge the eastern consumers to one of ridiculing the premier for "folding like a deck of cards" before the other premiers. Suddenly, the Liberals declared themselves to have been strongly supportive of Blakeney's strong "pro-Saskatchewan" stance leading up to the federal-provincial conference. When Blakeney failed to win freight rate or other concessions but agreed to keep the price of oil lower for domestic consumers despite the defeat, the Liberals said he had been weak.

It may have been good tactics for the party troops, but to many public observers, it was simply a transparent attempt to be on both sides of the issue.

During 1974, the Liberals continued their attacks on government centralization policies, despite NDP arguments that power was actually being decentralized through regional offices, more money to local governments, and more flexible policies. As the year wore on, the Liberals began to use Legislature debates or other speeches to outline the beginnings of the party's election platform for the following year. However, the emphasis was still on criticism, and increasingly the caucus showed itself often to be guided more by opportunism than by philosophy.

In the interests of appealing to voter constituencies, some glaring inconsistencies appeared. The government's $899 million budget was attacked for being too large while the Liberals were proposing expensive new programs such as senior citizen grants and more money to local governments. Steuart tried to score some points by calling for an inquiry when the government emasculated the powers of the Human Resources Development Agency in 1974, even though the Liberals had been highly critical of HRDA because its workers were acting as social organizers and activists among the poor and native people. And early in 1975 when the Legislature was called into session to order striking Saskatchewan Power Corporation employees back to work, Steuart at times appeared to be taking the side of the union just to attack the government.

Steuart saw his role throughout this period as keeping the party visible, the government on the defensive, and the electorate aware that there was an alternative. There is little doubt he accomplished some of that. The party did remain visible, and on some issues the Liberals effectively exposed government flaws, inconsistencies, and philosophical patterns. But some in the party also worried the overall effect was that the Liberals appeared simply negative and that after a while the voters would become immune to the overblown rhetoric and antileft exaggeration in which Steuart excelled.

Above all, the Opposition stances during those years were predictable. Members of the Liberal party who felt the party should be more positive said they were frustrated. "The trouble was that we put too much emphasis on scoring points and not enough on substantive issues," said one key party member. "The politicians were in control."

A senior government member took a similar stance. "We never thought of the Liberals as having a deep grasp of the issues in those years. In truth, we never really considered them a threat. Sometimes we worried that they might make an issue of some scandal allegation. But we didn't feel we had to have any special tactics to deal with them. Their responses were almost always predictable."

While Steuart was leading the day-to-day political fight, party strategists also wanted him to get exposure outside the province so he could be seen as a leader and potential statesman, as well as a scrappy politician. In the early years of his leadership, he had some notable successes.

The best performance came in February 1973 when he travelled to Toronto to address the Empire Club. It was vintage Steuart — a speech in which he played the role of the Prairie populist outraged over the treatment his area has received from the eastern business moguls. But rather than couching his message with the serious self-righteousness which afflicts many western spokesmen when they cross the Ontario-Manitoba border, Steuart slipped some one-liners into his sermon which had the crowd applauding.

He said eastern indifference toward the west must stop. He cited figures indicating poor prairie representation on the boards of companies which do huge business with the West and then complained that policies which affect the West are often made in the East with no consultation. "They don't consult us. They just charge whatever the market will bear and ignore us. I tell you and I warn them, time is running out and so is our patience."

Steuart's message was that economic power is travelling west and it was time central Canada woke up to the fact. The villains included the federal government, which did not buy enough goods in western Canada, but Steuart also took the opportunity to deny that the poor Liberal showing in Saskatchewan in the 1972 election was a backlash against the fact that Prime Minister Trudeau was French Canadian. He said westerners vote for different reasons than that, since Louis St. Laurent and John Diefenbaker were the two national leaders who had received the most support in Saskatchewan while they were in power. "The fact is our most successful politicians are either hell-raising Tories who hate the east or radical NDPs who hate everybody," he said.

Then Steuart travelled to Calgary with a sombre message for the Alberta Liberal Association: Liberalism would die in the West if Liberals did not work harder to be an alternative and to separate themselves from unpopular federal programs.

In July 1973, Steuart travelled to Vancouver for a national meeting of Liberals. He again played the champion of the West, attacking the federal Liberals for their policies and calling for special treatment for the Prairies to help them develop. Changes should include freight rate and tariff adjustments, better access to risk capital for the Prairies, and more federal spending to help stimulate the western economy. While many of the points were traditional western complaints, Steuart won wide media coverage and *Leader-Post* editorial support for his effort. "Mr. Steuart spoke for most westerners and most residents of Saskatchewan whatever their political leanings when he crisply and forcefully ticked off the major specific complaints of the West and challenged Mr. Trudeau and his colleagues to deal with them effectively," the newspaper said.

As the election drew closer, Steuart found himself increasingly tied down in Saskatchewan and unable to repeat his performances when they might have attracted more votes. However, his brief trips outside the province, and the media attention he aroused, proved to the leader and the party that adopting a traditional anti-East position was still good politics in the new Saskatchewan. Of course, Premier Blakeney had also learned that lesson and he found that route a far easier one to follow than Steuart did.

The issue of how to deal with Ottawa and the East was a thorny one for Steuart and the Liberals. Behind the scenes, efforts were underway to patch up the rifts between federal and provincial wings but in public it was not considered politically wise for the provincial members to appear to be too cozy with their federal colleagues. Ottawa is a traditional political enemy in Saskatchewan provincial politics, and any provincial politician becomes friendly with the "feds" at his own risk. It was a lesson Steuart knew well from his sixties days of fed-baiting with Premier Thatcher, and it was a position he knew he was going to have to get across to Saskatchewan voters.

The attempt started in late 1972 when Prime Minister Trudeau, recently almost defeated nationally and badly mauled in the West, was invited to the annual provincial Liberal convention. Steuart took the opportunity to publicly and privately lambaste the national leader for failing to understand the West and thereby hurting the party. After one meeting with the prime minister, he called him the "hippy dippy Frenchman," and the media saw it as an indication he would be his own man.

Three months later, the tactic surfaced again. This time the issue was federal failure to implement a small farms development program in Saskatchewan because of objections from the provincial government. Steuart called a news conference to blast the federal government for insensitivity to the West. "This is the first time since I've been leader that I have publicly criticized a federal cabinet minister and if we don't get some action in this regard, it will be the first of a series," he said. "Ottawa must realize the time for talk is over. Unless the federal government is willing to come to the aid of the Saskatchewan farmer in a material way, any hopes of improving federal Liberal representation from this province will never materialize."

In July at a national Liberal meeting, Steuart took the same message to national leaders and called for far more government attention for western problems. The entire campaign was a public relations triumph for the provincial leader.

There was also a dark side to the issue for Steuart. In part out of conviction and in part because of pressure from the increasingly-powerful federal organization in the province (including regular briefings for provincial caucus by Lang or one of his officials), Steuart often found himself defending federal positions that were unpopular in the province. When Lang called a producer vote on including rapeseed under the marketing powers of the Canadian Wheat Board and then weighed the vote against the wheat board, Steuart defended the move against NDP attack. Premier Blakeney chided him for defending the federal government in an attempt to win party favor and an eventual senate seat. Then, throughout the oil taxation debate in 1973-74, Steuart consistently sided with Ottawa and against the provincial government, often appearing to play apologist.

In most cases, Steuart bristled at any suggestion he was simply being a messenger boy for the federal government. But on one issue — debate over retention of the Crowsnest Pass freight rate subsidy for movement of prairie export grain by the railways — even Steuart later conceded he had been mistaken not to fight publicly with the federal Liberals.

The Crowsnest Pass rate is a fixed freight rate on grain movement, legislated in 1897 in part as a concession to western grain producers, dependent on selling their grain and, therefore, captive customers for the railways. It was part of the federal National Policy to attract agricultural settlement to the Prairies. Another side of the agreement gave the federal government, for the first time, the right to regulate freight rates charged by the CPR on western traffic. To win this important concession from the railway, Ottawa promised more than $3 million in grants to help finance construction of a CPR rail line from Alberta to resource-rich southeastern British Columbia, through the Crowsnest Pass. Although at the time the significant aspect of the agreement was considered to be the government right to regulate rail freight rates, the historically significant (and politically explosive) aspect of the agreement turned out to be the fixed grain rate. The statutory freight rate has remained at the 1897 level ever since, and legislative changes in the 1920s extended its application to other railways and included under its scope grain moving either to Thunder Bay (as in the original agreement) or to West Coast ports. As railway operating costs have escalated, the fixed producer rate has paid less and less of the cost of moving grain. By the mid-seventies, railways and government consultants said it was less than half and the shortfall was either absorbed by railways or paid by the federal government.

For most prairie farmers, the statutory rate is sacred, perceived as one of the few concessions they have received in a federal structure strongly weighted to protecting central Canadian business interests. The railways have long argued the Crow rate should be removed because it deprives them of needed revenue and leaves the system inflexible to the rationalization and capital renewal which could come with higher and variable rates. Using the excuse that grain movement is a losing proposition, the railways let their prairie rail network deteriorate over the years until many branch lines were almost impassable or totally abandoned by the seventies. By then, an increasingly vocal minority of farmers began to join the railways in clamoring for an end to the artificially low freight rates. They argued the benefits of the Crow rate could be paid directly to grain farmers but the railways needed more revenue to invest in their lines. They said the existence of the Crow rate retarded creation of secondary agricultural industries because it was more attractive to ship raw grain at low rates than to process it or feed it to cattle on the Prairies. Processed goods or meat are not covered by the low freight rates.

By the fall of 1974, Otto Lang had been convinced that if the Canadian grain handling system was to remain competitive, retention of the Crow rate would have to be reassessed. With advice from aides and government officials, he drew up a blueprint for change, including: abolition of the Crow rate; payment of a "Crow benefit" to producers to compensate them for any revenue lost through paying higher freight rates; controls on how much railways could charge, related to their costs; a comprehensive look at the rail network on the Prairies; a subsidy to producers forced to truck their grain because the local elevator had closed; variable freight rates to encourage rationalization of the grain handling system; and operation of a "Crow benefit" fund to be established by the government as a type of insurance scheme, paying more out to sectors with low returns in a given year. Lang was not ready to make his plan public yet and certainly not willing to make it government or party policy until he talked to producers about the idea. He was convinced the federal cabinet would support the idea, even though it meant increased government payments to grain producers. But he had to convince the cabinet that the change would be acceptable to prairie producers and perhaps even win the Liberals a few more friends on the Prairies.

Lang chose a meeting of the free-enterprise-oriented Canada Grains Council in Edmonton in October to propose the idea of a review of the Crow rate to see if the benefits could not be passed on to producers in a different way which would serve the industry better. While making it plain he thought the statutory rate was retarding growth in the West, Lang took no formal position. He asked the assembled agriculture representatives to begin a debate on the issue.

To Lang's logical mind, it may have been a reasonable and responsible proposal for a public discussion on a seventy-seven-year-old policy he thought was out of date. In Saskatchewan, with an election just months away, it was political dynamite. The wheat-dominated economy of the province had the most to lose from a change in the Crow rate, and the powerful Saskatchewan Wheat Pool, already feuding with Lang, was strongly opposed to any change. The provincial NDP quickly leaped on the Lang speech, and before long it had been distorted into a direct threat by the federal Liberals that the Crow rate would be destroyed, at a cost of hundreds of millions of dollars to Saskatchewan farmers. The NDP had been handed a perfect anti-fed issue to take into a campaign. The question was whether Steuart would let them make it a provincial issue as well.

He was in a quandary. He realized the NDP was distorting what Lang had said and he wanted to correct it. Yet he disagreed with both what Lang had said and when he had said it. (Several Saskatchewan party officials say they tried to dissuade Lang from making the Edmonton speech, but to no avail.) In the end, Steuart decided to stick by Lang and not to make it a public fight within the Liberal party. He thought a show of Liberal disunity would be bad for the party. The result was Steuart speeches defending Lang's proposal for a debate on the issue. Predictably, the NDP lumped the provincial Liberals into their Crow campaign and gleefully painted them as a party which would slaughter this sacred Saskatchewan cow.

The NDP argument was not factual, based on what the Liberals had said, but the perception was stronger than the reality, and it was an issue which haunted Steuart and the Liberals throughout the 1975 election campaign, eroding support in both country and city. Privately, provincial Liberals attacked their federal brothers, and Lang says he dropped a plan to try to sell his idea on Crow change to the West in part because of anguished pleas from Saskatchewan Liberals. His plan had been to stage a number of meetings in the next several years to sell the idea, keep it before the public, and, he hoped, win a consensus for change. But in the face of Pool and Liberal opposition, the plan was dropped and the campaign did not get off the ground.

Still, the damage had been done for provincial Liberals, and Lang later admitted at least two seats were lost by the Liberals in the subsequent provincial election because of his speech. Steuart was to consider his response one of the major mistakes of his leadership. "I should have taken Lang on," he said later. "I needed an issue to prove I was independent. Otto gave me one and I didn't take it. I was wrong." Many in his party agreed with him.

As the Legislature session drew to a close in April 1975, it was obvious an election was in the air.

Despite the flaws and tensions, party officials had some reasons for optimism. Organizing appeared to be going well and an attractive team of candidates had been fielded, polls showed NDP support flagging in some areas, and a policy platform had been developed which took the party beyond the days of existing simply to be anti-NDP. Party memberships had edged over 32,000, and officials told the media the party had close to $350,000 in the bank.[4]

Steuart felt ready for the battle, and the party was in as good a condition as he could make it. It would be his one chance to be premier, and while the fight would be tough with a well-entrenched government and the best economic times the province had ever known, he felt there was an outside chance the party could win. "I figured it would take a miracle, but in those days, a miracle seemed possible," he said.

There was one major problem with this vaguely optimistic outlook. In assessing their chances, the Liberals were almost totally ignoring the surging Progressive Conservative party under aggressive Saskatoon businessman Dick Collver. Until it was too late, the Liberals refused to believe the PCs would play any role in the election. They turned out to be the spoilers.

Considering the curious history of the provincial PC party, it isn't

---

[4] Total party assets were higher than this, of course. Party officials never included Thatcher's kitty, or what was left of it, in the figures they released to the public. The $350,000 was money collected and banked for the election campaign.

surprising the Liberals did not take them seriously. Although the province has been a federal Conservative stronghold since the 1957 win by local hero John Diefenbaker, the provincial party has seldom been relevant. Under J. T. M. Anderson, the Conservatives led a coalition government from 1929 to 1934, but when it collapsed, the party went into hiding. For more than two decades, the efforts of such leaders as Diefenbaker and Alvin Hamilton were insufficient to make it more than a fringe group with no Legislature representation.

In 1958, a businessman and farmer, Martin Pederson, took over the leadership from Hamilton, and the party went through a period of growth. By the 1964 election, it had thousands of members and won more than 19 percent of the popular vote — 127,410 votes. The Liberals won the election, and many credited the PCs with taking enough CCF votes to elect the Liberals. Pederson was the only PC elected, but it seemed like a foothold. However, during the next three years, he failed to consolidate organizationally the electoral gains the party had made, and when the 1967 provincial election was called unexpectedly early, the PCs were woefully ill-prepared. The party vote percentage dropped by half to 9.8 percent with 41,583 votes. Pederson lost his seat. The next year, he was replaced as leader and the party almost ceased to exist. In 1971, it ran sixteen candidates and won about 2 percent of the provincial vote.

When the party held a leadership convention in the spring of 1973, it seemed unusual that two candidates came forward, since the party had ceased to matter. Roy Bailey, a school superintendent from the Rosetown area, was the first declared candidate. A week before the convention, Saskatoon businessman Dick Collver announced he too was running and, surprisingly, he won the vote to become the new leader. The news was greeted with a yawn and a few chuckles around the province, but anyone who thought the party would remain static at the bottom was underestimating the energy, organizing ability, and ambition of the new leader.

Little was known about the thirty-seven-year-old Collver at the time. He had come to Saskatoon from Edmonton in 1965 and was employed by a family of Saskatoon doctors to manage their investments. He was an accountant and first appeared in the media when he dabbled in politics with an unsuccessful campaign for the mayoralty in 1971. In the spring of 1973 when a group of local Conservatives, including his employers, decided to try to revive the PC party, he decided to stand. His ambition was to be premier. His vehicle was a moribund party which could easily be molded into a stage for his views and a captive of his style. His platform was to be a brand of right-wing populism which concentrated on a return to more local control, tax reform to leave more money in taxpayers' pockets, and support for private enterprise. His style was tough and dictatorial, but through force of personality and an example of hard work, he attracted a small group of very dedicated organizers and supporters, many of them drop-outs from the Liberal party who were dissatisfied either with Steuart's style or with the perceived leftward swing in party policies.

Throughout 1973 and 1974, Collver travelled the province looking for candidates, stressing the need for an alternative to the NDP and Liberals, and gradually building some of the credibility which flows from media coverage. His policies were often vague and appeared ill-thought-out, but many found his confidence infectious and the prospect of a new face in politics attractive. Supporters of the federal PC party were being asked to be consistent in their provincial votes.

By the spring of 1975, Collver had managed to attract a full slate of candidates and he was pledging an all-out fight in the election.

The prospect of a serious PC threat still seemed incredible to many, however, and Liberals counted themselves among that group. In fact, the party had a history of not knowing exactly how to cope with the PCs. In the early sixties when both parties were gaining ground in the province, Ross Thatcher had outraged federal Liberals by proposing cooperation between Conservatives and Liberals to beat the CCF. Of course, Thatcher meant that Conservatives should join with the Liberals in their holy crusade, but he was also willing to promote some interparty dealing. PC Leader Pederson resisted the idea, but Thatcher did enough talking in public and the proposal seemed feasible enough that at least one PC official, the president of the Nipawin PC Association, resigned in protest before the 1964 election.

Pederson says Thatcher carried the idea of cooperation far enough that a meeting was arranged in Regina during the campaign to talk about it. He says Thatcher and two Liberals met Pederson and two Conservatives in a room rented by the Liberals. "The proposition was put to me by Ross that the Liberals would do what they could to see Conservatives elected in ten seats. In exchange, we had to agree to step out of a lot of seats the Liberals wanted. I refused." Pederson said Thatcher had prepared a list of ten specific ridings in which he was willing to see the Liberal candidate sacrificed. "That was how he was going to win government," Pederson said later. "I refused and the meeting ended." Then, according to the former PC leader, within two weeks he received a telephone call from a Saskatoon businessman, offering him a cheque for $87,000 to help fight the NDP "or for my own personal use." Pederson says he refused to take it, and although there was no mention of the Liberal proposal during the telephone conversation, he was left with the impression the two events were linked.

In 1967, the Thatcher decision to call an election before the PCs were organized effectively killed the party. Pederson argues it helped defeat the Liberals in 1971 by making that election a two-way fight which the Liberals could not win.

Throughout the first two years of the Collver leadership, the Liberal party remained ambivalent about the development. Party officials such as Sheard and Wilson felt the PCs could win up to 20 percent of the popular vote and mainly hurt the NDP. They were hoping for a modest but significant showing for the rejuvenated party.

However, their instincts and public opinion polls indicated little chance that would happen. "I found lots of voters saying they couldn't vote NDP and I took that as good news," said Rosthern candidate and former cabinet minister Allan Guy. "But they weren't putting on the rider that they might not vote for us either. And we didn't realize the threat."

It was a breakdown in political intelligence gathering which the party would later regret. A large pool of swing voters had developed, and they were unsure of the best way to register their dislike for what they considered flaws in the existing options. While the Liberals assumed the right wing had nowhere else to turn their discontent, these voters were increasingly turning their gaze to the revived Conservatives.

The reasons were complex and often localized. PC candidates such as Bob Larter in Estevan, Roy Bailey in Rosetown, and Dennis Ham in Swift Current were popular local figures who gave the local campaign credibility and attracted a personal following to the party. In the southeastern corner of the province, government oil and land policies were highly unpopular but the Liberals' often fuzzy policy alternative was not credible to the right-wing voters. On a provincial basis, the single most important factor was the drive and hard work of Collver and his entourage. He sensed public disaffection with both the NDP and the federal and provincial Liberals and was able to tie them together in the public mind by highlighting the bickering between the two "old line parties" in the previous four years.

Collver's policy ideas were usually vague and often illogical, but he represented a dynamic, strong-leader image which appealed to many voters cynical about the other two parties. By building a credible organization and running a high-profile campaign, he convinced many federal PC voters that they should give the party a chance provincially. For an increasingly affluent and conservative population, he offered general promises of less government, more local control, and less partisanship. This approach tapped a growing rural mood of self-reliance. The promise of more local control appealed to voters looking for a way to deal with some powerful biases and perceived problems such as insensitive bureaucracy and welfare abuse.

Collver and the Conservatives were beginning to raise expectations in a growing segment of the population which felt the NDP offered too much centralized power and the Liberals offered no attractive alternative or simply more of the same.

A. H. (Hammy) McDonald opens the provincial Liberal campaign March 3, 1956. Three years later, McDonald was deposed as party leader to make way for Ross Thatcher. (Sask. Archives: Star-Phoenix Collection)

Relations between Saskatchewan Liberals and the federal Liberal party have often been strained. Nevertheless, in 1960 the provincial leader Ross Thatcher (left) and the federal leader Lester Pearson (right) posed together with Saskatchewan's Liberal patriarch, Jimmy Gardiner. (Sask. Archives: Star-Phoenix Collection)

In 1970, Premier Ross Thatcher opened the new education building at the University of Saskatchewan, Saskatoon. (Sask. Archives: Star-Phoenix Collection)

Less than a year later, in June 1971, Ross Thatcher was waging his last campaign. (Sask. Archives: Star-Phoenix Collection)

Otto Lang was dean of law at the University of Saskatchewan before he went into federal politics and joined the cabinet of Pierre Elliot Trudeau. (Sask. Archives: Star-Phoenix Collection)

During the late sixties and the seventies, Otto Lang dominated federal politics in Saskatchewan. (Sask. Archives: Star-Phoenix Collection)

The Liberal leadership convention in 1971 followed in the wake of an NDP victory in that year's provincial election and the sudden death of the former leader Ross Thatcher. (Sask. Archives: Star-Phoenix Collection)

Dave Steuart (center) was one of three candidates running for leader. (Sask. Archives: Star-Phoenix Collection)

On the second ballot, the field narrowed down to Dave Steuart and his fellow MLA Cy MacDonald. (Sask. Archives: Star-Phoenix Collection)

Dave Steuart was elected leader of the Saskatchewan Liberal party December 11, 1971. (Sask. Archives: Star-Phoenix Collection)

Tony Merchant ran a slick media-oriented campaign in his 1976 bid for leadership of the Saskatchewan Liberal party. (Saskatoon Star-Phoenix photo)

Ted Malone was the candidate favored by the middle-of-the-road Liberals in the 1976 leadership race. (Saskatoon Star-Phoenix photo)

In December 1976, Ted Malone took over as leader of the Saskatchewan Liberal party but his moment of triumph was brief. The party he inherited was badly divided, demoralized, and short of money. (The Leader-Post, Regina, Sask.)

In the 1978 provincial election, Ted Malone and the provincial Liberals lost every Legislature seat they had taken into the election and garnered less than 14 percent of the total vote. (The Leader-Post, Regina, Sask.)

In the federal election of May 22, 1979, every Liberal candidate was defeated, including the powerful minister of transport, Otto Lang. (Saskatoon Star-Phoenix photo)

Chapter Nine

THE 1975 ELECTION CAMPAIGN: THE RACE FOR POWER

The election campaign officially began May 14, 1975, when Premier Blakeney emerged from a cabinet meeting in the Legislature building to announce a June 11 vote.

Within hours, all three parties were announcing their plans for campaigning and leaders' tours, and putting into action schedules which had been developed over the winter.

The New Democrats would send Blakeney around the province in a rented Saskatchewan Transportation Company bus with the same driver who piloted the bus during the successful 1971 campaign. They would campaign on leadership strength, the need for strong resource management policies, an expanded welfare state structure, and tax breaks for voters. The government record of the past four years would be an issue, Blakeney said, but he would be more interested in battling the federal government over agriculture, transportation, and resource taxation policies which were affecting Saskatchewan. The NDP was asking provincial voters for a mandate to negotiate with Ottawa over energy and what level of taxation both governments should apply to the oil industry.[1]

The New Democrats were going into the campaign with a strong case for a renewed mandate. During their first term in power, they had made popular moves such as ending medicare premiums, creating a denticare program for school children, and attempting to deal with underdevelopment in northern Saskatchewan and high land prices in farming areas. The party had also had the good fortune to be elected to office when farm and

---

[1] It was the era when federal and provincial governments were scrambling to get a cut of increasing oil prices, and by 1975, both Ottawa and Regina were applying taxes which the oil industry said were taking more than 100 percent of its profits. Blakeney argued Ottawa was using its taxing power to challenge provincial ownership rights over resources.

natural resource sectors were poised for a period of strong growth, and in the previous four years Saskatchewan had become moderately wealthy with tens of millions of dollars building up in government surpluses. There was also more money to fund social programs, and in many cases, taxes and utility charges were lower than they had been several years before.

However, it was also clear the party could not maintain the phenomenal 55 percent of the vote received in 1971. It was the job of the Opposition parties to present themselves as the worthy beneficiaries of the disenchantment which was bound to come.

The Progress·.e Conservatives announced they would campaign throughout the province. Leader Dick Collver would travel by car and van to most areas, and while he publicly predicted a Tory victory, privately party officials hoped for ten or twelve seats. Realistically, if the party won any seats it would be a major breakthrough, and Collver's campaign was virtually a no-lose situation. The party announced it would campaign on a platform of vague promises to get sectors of society working together again. Government power would be reduced and the private sector enhanced, smoother labor relations and a more equitable arrangement with the resource companies would be negotiated, which would result in adequate tax income yet encourage increased development.

Primarily, it was a promise of a change of pace in political life, fewer political divisions, and less government.

The Liberals announced they would send Steuart around the province by van and plane. The party actually kicked off its campaign several weeks before the official campaign began by staging a giant rally in Saskatoon. Close to 500 supporters were bussed to the Centennial Auditorium, the sixty-one candidates were introduced, and the election platform was officially unveiled. Steuart called it a blueprint to open up the province to more private investment, higher corporate tax revenues, and reduced government power. An estimated $200 million worth of promises — ranging from minimum incomes for senior citizens and more money for local governments to extension of the government-subsidized grain freight rate to cover other agricultural products as well — would be funded by increased government tax revenues drawn from a booming private sector.

The public pitch for votes was supplemented by a private strategy which party officials hoped would give them an outside chance of winning. They would concentrate attacks on government growth and land bank policies, because private polls showed these were two issues bothering voters. They would concentrate on the Liberal candidates as a strong team, rather than stressing Steuart's leadership, because the polls also showed Blakeney more popular than Steuart. They would try to appeal to wavering NDP voters by painting that party as a group of power-hungry politicians out of touch with the dreams of the CCF founders. And they would largely ignore the Conservatives, in part because they did not consider the PCs a threat and in part because they feared giving the Tories credibility by criticizing them.

The key to the campaign would be a heavy barrage of slick media advertising which would concentrate on attacks on the government during the first half of the campaign and then switch to positive Liberal proposals during the last two weeks before the vote. During this time, the sixty-one-year-old Steuart would maintain a rigorous personal campaign schedule, organized in part to show that although he was the oldest of the three leaders, he was as fit as the other two. Campaign organizers also hoped more personal exposure would show the public a more temperate Steuart than the negative politician so often portrayed in the media.[2]

The advertising and travelling would be a costly exercise, but unlike the Conservatives, money was not a problem for the Liberal party. The fund-raising trips and dinners, payments from the federal Liberal party, and the remains of Thatcher's kitty provided the party with the funds it needed to print the platforms and pamphlets and pay for much of the advertising before the election writ was issued and before income and expenses had to be claimed. Once the official campaign began, the push for funds increased, and in that month, more than $200,000 was received by the Liberals. Based on documents filed later with the provincial electoral office, most of the donations were under $100 and the identity of the donor did not have to be revealed. However, some traditional corporate sources were more generous in their support for Liberal resource or business policies. Oil and mining companies such as Dome Petroleum of Calgary, Dennison Mines of Toronto, and Pacific Petroleums of Calgary donated several thousand dollars each. The Winnipeg grain company, N. M. Paterson and Sons, also supported the Liberals with dollars, as did Saskatchewan companies such as Westbank Industries ($1500) and Redi-Mix of Regina ($2625).

With money available, an extensive set of policies, and polls indicating some NDP weaknesses, senior Liberal officials began the campaign with some optimism, although they knew it would be a tough fight. "There were only 36 ridings in the province the Liberals could even think of winning," one campaign organizer said later. "We had our work cut out for us."

In the early days of the campaign, the electioneering appeared to be going well, although there were two early setbacks. Any thought that the election could be fought on policy, rather than leadership, was quickly dispelled when NDP ads began to promote Blakeney as a key issue. Reluctantly, the Liberals had to face the challenge. "With Mr. Steuart's agreement, we wanted to play down leadership and play up policy," said Steuart aide Jim Roche. "But when the NDP began to stress leadership as an issue, we had to respond." It was a battleground on which the Liberals did not expect to win.

The NDP decision to stress federal issues and to attack federal Liberal policies was also a setback for provincial Liberals. They had hoped to avoid

---

[2] One factor which gave campaign directors headaches was the fear that Steuart might lose his Prince Albert seat. He had to be scheduled into Prince Albert as often as possible, and this sometimes disrupted campaign trips to other ridings.

the debate over federal-provincial Liberal ties, but the NDP move was inevitable. It put Steuart in a difficult position, considering the unpopularity of federal Liberal policies in Saskatchewan and the tensions which were increasingly evident within the party over that issue. Should he respond on behalf of the federal Liberals in fear voters would assume an unanswered charge was true and that Liberals were all alike? Or should he ignore the attacks and risk having the federal Liberals respond, appearing to interfere in the election campaign when provincial Liberals were trying to prove they were independent? It was a dilemma which Steuart never quite resolved, and on both resource taxation and the Crowsnest Pass freight rate, the federal connection would haunt him throughout the campaign.

His initial response illustrated the dilemma. The day the campaign opened, Steuart challenged Blakeney to leave federal issues and policies alone. The next day, he showed his own willingness to lean on the federal connection for his own advantage when he prematurely announced a $55-million federal-provincial agreement to provide improved northern communications in the province. Steuart hoped to limit NDP mileage from the agreement by announcing it first. Instead, his move showed provincial voters how close federal and provincial Liberals could be when it suited their purposes.

The first two weeks of the campaign saw Steuart travelling the province, alternately attacking and promising. He said Liberals would attract three or four new potash mines to the province, make more money available to local governments, improve nurses' working conditions, lower oil prices, and introduce a subsidized drug plan. One of his more controversial promises came in Saskatoon when he casually pledged renter grants similar to property improvement grants for homeowners. The party had not approved the idea and it was not included in the official platform. Many candidates heard about it for the first time on their radios and soon found themselves defending a give-away they were unfamiliar with and in many cases opposed to. For Steuart, the promise proved to be a mixed blessing.

Along with the promises, there were the attacks. Steuart was always best on the attack and he often had party true-believers standing to applaud as he called the NDP everything from incompetent and impotent to crooked. In Preeceville, one moment of emotional rhetoric hurt party chances to win the labor vote. In the middle of a speech about problems in the province, Steuart shouted: "Give us the power and we'll straighten out those unions." It was a message Liberal hard-liners wanted to hear about Big Labor, but when the next day's newspapers carried the quote, visions of Bill 2 and the antilabor tactics of the previous Liberal government began to appear. Steuart later claimed he had been misinterpreted and he had only meant he would change the Trade Union Act to give union members the right to criticize their own unions without fear of expulsion or reprimand. However, despite the backtracking, the damage had been done, and if many union members had any doubt about supporting the NDP, that likely ended it.

Although the attacks were part of the party strategy — and probably the aspect which best suited Steuart's style — party officials soon began to worry that the strategy was backfiring. The attacks were receiving media coverage and, increasingly, the image of the Liberal campaign was a negative one. Roche says as this became obvious, Steuart's staff tried to convince him to tone down his rhetoric. "He said he couldn't," Roche said. "He said 'I am what I am.' "

Midway through the campaign, Steuart announced a change of style to accentuate the positive. Party officials hoped it would be a turning point, accompanied by a change in advertising content from criticism to program proposals. "From now on, we're going to be talking about what we're going to do," Steuart told reporters in Swift Current. For a few days, it seemed the change had been made. Steuart stepped up his announcements of policy and promises, and in Shaunavon, a southern Saskatchewan farming community, he put together his vision of the future in one of the most philosophical and emotional speeches of the campaign. He said a Liberal Saskatchewan would be filled with companies opening new plants and investing money to create jobs, increase tax revenues, and encourage the creation of spin-off industries in small towns. "We have been offered a chance to do this because our raw materials are in demand now, but the NDP has passed up the opportunity," he said. "That is why this election is a crossroads for the province."

The speech drew warm response from the packed hall, but the greatest cheer came when Steuart vowed a Liberal government would deal "sternly" with anyone on welfare who refused to work once job training had been given. "They'll be cut off," he said and the crowd roared its approval.

As the campaign progressed, the pattern continued that the best crowd response and media coverage came when Steuart was criticizing. The image remained, and to compound the problem, the planned switch of ads from negative to positive was not made and media consumers continued to be exposed to clever but negative advertising.

The foul-up in ad switching was just one of a number of organizational flaws which began to appear in the campaign before it was half over.

Part of the problem was that the party's system of voter intelligence was totally inadequate. Officials in Regina central office were looking for accurate reports from local campaign officials so they could have a reading on how the campaign was progressing and so they could make decisions on where to assign their scarce campaigning resources. Instead, they were getting rosy reports from candidates and their managers which were often intended to encourage local workers rather than to give central office an accurate assessment. "The party wasn't as well organized as it should have been when we needed it," Executive Director Sheard conceded later. In large part, it was his job to make sure that the organization was in shape.

While good news was pouring in from the Liberal front, the private opinion polls were telling another, more pessimistic tale. Decision Making Information Canada of Edmonton was providing frequent riding or area samples, and two weeks into the campaign, these readings began to show a Progressive Conservative presence. Many of the voters who had been undecided and were considered likely Liberal supporters were deciding to try the Conservatives and their rhetoric of change. Liberal planners were thrown into a panic. "The Tories were not really a factor until well into the campaign and by then, we didn't know what to do with them," said Sheard.

The media were not as undecided. Many reporters felt the Conservative rise was the developing story of the election campaign and the coverage made the Liberals bitter. Before the campaign began, the two major dailies in the province — the *Saskatoon Star-Phoenix* and the *Regina Leader-Post* — had decided to send a reporter with each leader for an equal amount of time. The newspaper philosophy was that until the voters have their say, each party has an equal right to get its message across. To downplay the Conservatives because of their 1971 showing would be prejudging the voter mood, since the PCs had a full slate and were campaigning as hard as the Liberals and NDP. Liberals complained that this policy gave the PCs more credibility than they deserved and that the swing to the Conservatives was the result of the media attention.

Relations with the media were strained even more after Liberals complained about a decision by both the Regina and Saskatoon newspapers to create election pages inside the papers, rather than playing election stories on the front page. "You only beat the government on Page 1," Steuart complained. "When I saw the way the newspapers were treating the election, I knew no miracle would happen." Privately, Steuart took his charges a step further. He complained that the newspapers were playing down the election because they had decided the NDP was going to win and with heavy government advertising a media mainstay, it was in their interests not to affect that likelihood. Newspaper spokesmen like then *Star-Phoenix* editor Stirling King hotly deny the charge. "When a politican can't make it, he blames the press," said King. "We never sat down and decided the Liberals couldn't win and let that influence our coverage."

As the organizational problems mounted and polls showed Liberals running behind the government and Conservatives starting to gain, Liberal leaders decided it had become a race for second place. Steuart says by mid-campaign he had decided the party should begin to concentrate money, workers, and efforts in ridings where they had a chance. "I thought by then there were 20 or 25 we could win. I told the election committee to concentrate on them." It became one of the crucial errors in the Liberal campaign. The order was not carried out.

Steuart said by the end of May with eleven campaign days left, he assumed the plan had been put into effect and weaker ridings had been abandoned to free more people for work in possible-win ridings, including the fifteen seats held by the party in the previous Legislature. A rally in

Saskatoon on May 30 dispelled that idea. Officials from Meadow Lake, where Hal Coupland seemed to be in trouble, told Steuart no one from other ridings had been in to help. After the encounter, Steuart confronted Sheard. "The election committee obviously hadn't been doing it. I got excuses and that's all," he said later.

That night, Steuart also learned something about the weaknesses in his own leadership. "That's where Ross Thatcher would have been tough and I wasn't," he said. "At that point, I should have ordered people around but I didn't."

It was clearly a major flaw in the organization, but other party officials suggest it may have been broader than simply Steuart's reluctance to order Sheard around. They suggest it was a natural outgrowth of the mood which Steuart and the new leadership had tried to instill in the party. There would be less dictatorial rule from the top, they had said. There would be more authority at the local level. When it came time to tell constituencies they were being written off, no one wanted to be the person to admit the new philosophy had not worked. After the election, Sheard conceded the movement to encourage development at the constituency level may have led to some of the problems. "We tried to build our organization generally and that may have been one of our big mistakes," he said. "We spread ourselves too thin."

Even as these problems became apparent within the organization, the public campaign continued with gusto. Steuart continued his travels, his promises, and his attacks. In Swift Current on June 4, he warned: "Any government powerful enough to do anything for you is also powerful enough to do anything to you." Crowds remained large and appeared enthusiastic.

The Liberal campaign ended with a giant rally at the Centre of the Arts in Regina. An estimated 4,000 to 5,000 people turned out to hear predictions of victory. The rally was broadcast live throughout the province as an advertisement, and Steuart promised if the Liberals were elected, he would call an early Legislature session to implement many of the campaign promises. The only major hitch of the rally was a bomb threat which disrupted proceedings temporarily. It gave the Liberal leader a last chance to make a questionable charge against the NDP on province-wide radio. He accused the New Democrats of illegal and intimidating tactics (implying the bomb threat was their work) and ended with: "We're not frightened. We're angry." It may have been good boosterism for the party faithful, but many non-committed voters may have wondered about the charge.

Then, the campaign was over. Figures filed with the provincial electoral office indicate more than $1 million had been spent on the campaign by all parties. Official expenses filed indicated spending by the provincial organization totalled $169,714 for the Liberals, $168,591 for the PCs, and $164,971 for the NDP. Hundreds of thousands more could be spent at the constituency level, and expenditures before the writ was issued were not included. It had officially been the most expensive campaign in Saskatchewan history and one of the most exhausting. As the June 11 voting day dawned on the province, the three leaders stationed themselves around the province to await voter judgment on their record and the last hectic twenty-eight days of campaigning. Steuart was in Prince Albert, Blakeney in Regina, and Collver in Saskatoon, ready to fly to his northeastern riding of Nipawin when results were known.

Within an hour of the 8:00 P.M. poll closing, the trend was clear. The NDP would win with a reduced but healthy majority. The Liberals would remain the official Opposition, but with a substantially reduced share of the popular vote. The Conservatives would be a strong third force with a sizable voter following.

The final count was: NDP, thirty-nine; Liberals, fifteen; PCs, seven. The popular vote of the NDP dropped from 55 percent to 40 percent. Liberal strength was down from 43 percent to 32 percent. Conservative strength rose from 2 percent to 28 percent.

On the surface of the electoral results, the Liberals appeared to have held their own. They retained the fifteen-seat total won in the 1971 election despite the onslaught of the Conservatives and the record of the NDP. More importantly, the party had elected a number of new, young, promising candidates. Ten of the fifteen were first-time MLAs and two of the remaining five — Jack Wiebe and Ted Malone — had first been elected in by-elections after the 1971 vote. Of the remaining three, only Steuart and Cy MacDonald were Thatcher government veterans. Gary Lane had first been elected in 1971 and remained one of the younger MLAs.[3]

However, the losses were clearly greater than the gains. Four previous Liberal seats — Hal Coupland (Meadow Lake), Allan Guy (Rosthern), John Gardner (Moosomin), and Tom Weatherald (Souris-Cannington) — had been lost and three of them were won by Conservatives. The traditional Liberal stranglehold on rural southeastern Saskatchewan had been shattered by the PCs. The 32-percent vote was one of the lowest the Liberals had ever received, and with just four percentage points between the Liberals and PCs, the battle for second place had clearly just begun. The final voting results showed Liberals ran second in twenty-seven seats. The PCs were second in nineteen, including four of the Liberal victories.

The governing NDP had also suffered a setback. Their working majority had been reduced from twenty-nine at dissolution to sixteen after the election. Three cabinet ministers and a handful of MLAs had been defeated. But they had the consolation of winning government again and the renewed mandate Blakeney had asked for to negotiate with the federal government.

---

[3] New Liberal MLAs elected were: Sonny Anderson (Shaunavon), Stuart Cameron (Regina South), Linda Clifford (Wilkie), Evelyn Edwards (Saskatoon Sutherland), Neil McMillan (Kindersley), Tony Merchant (Regina Wascana), Roy Nelson (Assiniboia-Gravelbourg), Glen Penner (Saskatoon Eastview), Bill Stodalka (Maple Creek), and Colin Thatcher (Thunder Creek).

The Liberals had no such consolation, other than the vague hope that the new caucus would be able to do better than the last one. With a new alternative on the right, that job would be more complicated than ever.

Election night hit the Liberals hard. Unlike 1971, they had not expected to win. But they also had not expected the strong showing of the Conservatives and the obvious challenge to their position as the main alternative to the NDP.

In Prince Albert, Steuart found himself winning with an 853 vote margin, one of his largest ever. Yet despite the good local news, he told reporters the buoyant economy, the rise of the PCs, and his own leadership were the reasons for the poor showing. He hinted that he wouldn't be around to lead the party through another election and he vowed not to be a "kingmaker" if the party looked for a new leader. He also credited himself with keeping the Liberal party alive for the past four years and he took a shot at the media for giving the PCs credibility "just because they were a new thing."

The press was not long in responding. The next day, the *Saskatoon Star-Phoenix*, once a supporter of the Thatcher government and more recently an Otto Lang booster, editorially blamed the Liberal misfortunes on Steuart. "We do not mean to be unkind to Mr. Steuart, whom we and many others in Saskatchewan hold in deep respect. But we are bound to say he was not able to generate sufficient fire power to attract a great deal of attention. Mr. Steuart also suffers from public association with the late Premier Ross Thatcher, who in spite of his often wise approach to government, was almost angrily ousted from office in the 1971 provincial election." It was hardly a vicious putdown of the Liberals, but the editorial ended with a far more pointed, if mute, criticism of Steuart's leadership record. It said one of Thatcher's best techniques was his ability to keep provincial and federal Liberal wings separated and often feuding. "That policy may have to be dusted off and re-implemented by a provincial Liberal organization bent on taking power." In other words, Steuart's attempts to reconcile the two wings of the Liberal party may have been at the expense of provincial aspirations.

It was one of the questions Liberals would be asking themselves in the following months as they tried to pinpoint the reason for their failure.

A number of explanations were soon being offered — Steuart had been too negative, the organization had let the party down, many of the candidates had not worked hard enough, the platform was too left, wing to be sold as a Liberal document. All these theories had their defenders and detractors within the party as they looked for lessons from the failure.

Had the policy formulation process been a success? Cy MacDonald complained that the final product was much too-left wing for his liking. "We tried to out-NDP the NDP," he said. Newly-elected MLA Roy Nelson agreed. "Too often, it appeared members of the Liberal Party wanted to shift to the left and did not follow the philosophy of the Liberals," he said later. "We had entirely too many give-aways, in my opinion, and while the policy could have been implemented, few of the swing vote believed our platform." Others felt the policy was a good effort, but it had not been sold properly. Steuart had spent too much time attacking the NDP or making promises not included in the platform, instead of selling the official program.

The organization was also a major flaw (although the Liberals were far more organized than the PCs). The election committee and central office had clearly not exercised the required control over the final effort. Steuart also conceded that while he had attracted new, young candidates in many areas, he was not able to renew the base of the party in the same way. Many of the workers in the 1975 campaign had been around since Thatcher's days. They had fought one too many battles. "We had a good organization but it had been to the well once too often," Steuart said. "It just didn't have the enthusiasm."

There were other, obvious causes for the Liberal setback. Federal Liberal policies were largely unpopular, Liberal attempts in the previous four years to nurture the traditional right wing while reaching ever further into the government give-away bag were not believable, and the Conservatives, with a dynamic leader and no record to defend, appealed to the affluent and conservative rural voter.

The overall problem, however, was credibility, and for many, that meant Dave Steuart. He ran a spirited campaign, worked hard, and had led the party through some important rebuilding steps during the previous four years. But for many, he was not a serious contender. He was a relic from the discredited past.

In retrospect, Steuart defended the type of campaign he ran, disputing the charges of excess negativism and complaining that it was being misrepresented. "Relative to most campaigns, it was positive," he said. "But I do tend to be an old-fashioned political fighter. I enjoy the heat of battle. I do think governments are defeated."

In that attitude lay one of the seeds of Liberal problems in 1975. Despite all the effort at policy creation, the politics of positive thinking, and the talk of "new look Liberals," the party was still being led by a man who believed in old-style politicking. In an election campaign, the leader and his speeches set the tone for the party image, and at least in style and rhetoric, Steuart ran a Thatcher campaign in 1975. The similarity between Liberal speeches of the early sixties and 1975 is striking. They both lamented economic stagnation, the lack of development, and the "deadening hand of socialism" under the NDP. The answer was to bring outside investors to spend their money, create jobs, and take the profits back to their head offices. Tax revenues left behind would fund social programs.

In the early sixties, the approach worked and the Liberals were elected. In 1975, it was a vastly different world. Economic times were good, Blakeney was a stronger and more formidable opponent than Woodrow Lloyd had been in 1964, and after a decade of the welfare state nationally, Big Government was not as emotional an issue as it had once been.

In 1975's affluent, self-assured Saskatchewan, the Thatcher style of politics and paranoia seemed oddly out of place. Many voters were willing to believe that the NDP was not the best choice to lead them into a more conservative and stable future, but they were not willing to accept Steuart's conspiracy theories, negativism, or new-found faith in benevolent government. His major deviation from the Thatcher line was to patch up differences with the federal Liberals and to offer some expensive programs funded with expected development boom spin-offs. His federal reconciliation was not acceptable and his welfare state not believable.

PC leader Collver was able to benefit from these flaws. He also offered the image of strength and a thinly-veiled streak of authoritarianism which may have appealed. Ironically, Steuart's reaction against the strong-arm tactics of Thatcher may in the end have been one more political flaw.

Months after the election, Liberals were still agonizing over the Tories and what could be done to stop them. No consensus developed, and the implications of that vacuum would surface later when the party would be forced to cope with the Conservatives as a real and growing threat to their limited voter base. After decades of aiming all their guns at the hated left side of the political spectrum, the Liberals were finding it difficult to cope with a threat from the right, which they had always taken for granted as theirs.

In the aftermath of the election, it was inevitable that Steuart's presence in the party would begin to fade as the search began for a new leader. The question was not if he would quit but 'when' and how messy the transition would be. Although he would technically be leader until a replacement was named, Steuart was a spent force in the party with one last job — to act as a teacher and sometimes an inspiration for the new MLAs until they felt comfortable with the system and were ready to pick a new leader.

It was also inevitable that during the next year assessments of Steuart's leadership years would be made. Leadership candidates would try to score points by telling the world what they would have done differently. Bitter party workers would look for someone else to blame.

Steuart offered four views of his leadership years. On the last campaign: "It was a far better campaign than we have been given credit for. There were just too many things to overcome." On his personal style: "I think the younger people are not prepared to accept the harsh black and white that existed in politics in the Fifties and into the mid-Sixties. The younger generation want a more reasoned approach. They are not prepared to listen to charges like 'threat of socialism.' Labels don't mean much to them." On his personal disappointment: "I'm a realist. I had a chance. That's more than most people get." On his legacy to the party: "My legacy is that I kept the party together, kept it sound financially and helped the Tories get a foothold. I can't step away from that reality."

Chapter Ten

A PARTY DIVIDED

The immediate aftermath of the election for the Liberal party was lethargy bred of disappointment. There were few public outbursts and no public bloodbath of recrimination about the election loss, but there was also little enthusiasm or commitment to begin to rebuild.

Many Liberals set their minds to the causes of the defeat and the basic strength of the party. Memberships were high because it had been an election year, and although party coffers were beginning to deplete, the party still had hundreds of thousands of dollars at its disposal. But would the memberships be renewed and the money keep coming in to fund the rebuilding necessary in the next four years? Were opponents of the NDP willing to give the Liberals another chance, or would they turn in increasing numbers to the Conservatives?

These were troubling questions which touched none more than Dave Steuart as he contemplated his failure. Obviously, he was not the person to lead the rebuilding. He felt he must make that clear, to save young Turks in the party the energy they would probably expend pushing him out. But he also concluded he had to stay for a while to teach the new MLAs the system and give the potential replacements a chance to develop their followings and to prove themselves in political battle with the NDP and the PCs. The last major effort of this thorough-going party man would be to prepare the party for his own demise.

On June 13, two days after the election, he announced formally that he would be stepping down, but he would stay on as leader until the party was ready to choose a successor.

Not long afterwards, he made the first tentative move to look after his personal future as well. During the summer, he told Transport Minister Lang he would be interested in some day filling a Senate seat. Although Steuart says he received no clear response from Lang and did not expect one then, the seed had been planted.[1]

---

[1] In any campaign for a Saskatchewan Senate seat, Lang was the man to see first. As

The future leadership of the party was one of the main points of political speculation during summer, in a province which had had its fill of politics for a while. Newspaper stories speculated Steuart would stay on until the next year and that the major potential successors were Regina lawyers and MLAs Tony Merchant, Ted Malone, and Gary Lane. None were commenting on the possibility, but in one speech Merchant made it plain he thought a new leader could do better in some ways. He complained that Steuart had been too negative and that had helped bring the party down.

The summer passed quietly, except for minor flurries when the NDP faced charges it had delayed Saskatchewan Power Corporation gas rate hikes until after the election and when Steuart began to issue weekly written questions to the government. The latter was an attempt to stir some publicity for the Liberals, but when the government ignored the questions and the media grew indifferent or hostile to the idea, the attempt was abandoned.

As summer turned into fall, all appeared relatively quiet within the party, but beneath the surface two issues were coming to life which would soon shake the party hierarchy and badly divide it. The blow-ups clearly showed the tenuous hold a lame duck leader has on his party. More significantly, they showed that Steuart's four-year attempt to unite the party had produced at best a fragile union, always with the potential to break down.

The first crisis developed from a seemingly harmless beginning. Shortly after the election, several Liberals, including Merchant, circulated within the party a proposal for a new type of leadership convention. It was called "Liberally" and proposed that all card-carrying Liberals be given a direct vote when the next leadership change was being made. The vote would take several days and members would vote by a closed-circuit system from seven or eight major centres across the province. It was billed as a way to democratize the process and its proponents argued the electronic hardware existed to carry it off.

Party leaders were interested enough that at a July 12 executive meeting, a committee was established to study the proposal and to report its findings to an executive meeting in September. Several weeks before the scheduled September 19 meeting, Merchant talked to reporters about his idea (and with an eye for publicity, he claimed much of the credit for it). Reporters called Steuart and he told them that any idea to give members

---

the province's only federal cabinet minister, he would have a strong say in any appointments to fill federal vacancies from the province. At the time, there was a Senate vacancy. Some Steuart critics believe he made the first approaches on a Senate seat long before the election, in return for efforts to end provincial Liberal antagonism toward the federal Liberals. Steuart denies it and there appears no evidence to support the claim.

more control was a good one. If it came before the fall convention, said Steuart, "I will speak in favor of it."

Suddenly, Liberally was a major divisive issue within the party. A group of MLAs and executive members felt the plan was a thinly disguised attempt to boost a Merchant leadership run by giving the cities of Saskatoon and Regina greater say in selecting the next leader. (They reasoned that the party would have more members voting from those two cities and they were the power bases of Lang and his brother-in-law Merchant.) They saw Steuart's public endorsement as an attempt by the retiring leader to favor a Merchant candidacy. Another group was offended simply because Steuart and Merchant had broken party confidence and protocol by making a proposal public before it had been judged by the party. The two groups began efforts to short-circuit the plan. Executive members, led by Vice-President Donna Welke of Regina and Liberal Women's President Shirley Black of Regina, began to organize opposition. An informal meeting of some executive members days after the story appeared drew from Treasurer John Embury an estimate that the Merchant plan would cost close to $300,000 to implement.

Simultaneously, MLA Gary Lane, long a Steuart opponent and an antifederal Liberal, began to contact other MLAs and found some of them also opposed to the proposal or the way it was unveiled. A regular caucus meeting had been planned for mid-September in Regina, and before the meeting a group of at least seven MLAs met at the Vagabond Motor Inn to discuss it. Despite Lane's disclaimers, several at the meeting began to feel part of an attempt by Lane to discredit Merchant and Steuart for his own leadership ambitions. Others resolved to fight the issue at caucus. Meanwhile, the executive had moved its scheduled September 19 meeting ahead a week to hold a special meeting after caucus, with Steuart in attendance.

While all the planning was going on, Steuart remained unaware of the furor he had set off. He arrived at the caucus meeting expecting to discuss party fortunes and strategy for the fall. Instead he faced a stream of questions and complaints about his comments on Liberally. Merchant wasn't there, so Steuart took the brunt of it. Although MLA recollections of the caucus meeting vary slightly, it is agreed that several MLAs, led by Lane, wanted a commitment from Steuart that he would drop the issue and suggested a press release be issued retracting support for Liberally. Steuart took the offensive. "I blew up. I told them if they condemned the press release, they were censuring me." Steuart stormed out of the meeting in a rage, after telling them if they wanted him to resign, he would. With no target to shoot at and some MLAs getting edgy about being too harsh on Steuart, the issue died.

Later that day, the leader went to the emergency executive meeting and found more of the same. Some executive members complained about the Liberally comments and Welke produced a letter she proposed be sent to Liberal members which condemned the Steuart and Merchant comments as "premature" and called the Liberally idea an apparent "Merchant-Lang proposal." The letter said Steuart's comments had been "not in the best interest of our Liberal party" and any further public discussion of the issue before it went to convention would be "manipulative and irresponsible." The executive amended the letter to take out the reference to Lang's influence on the idea, and eventually it was tabled without decision. Again Steuart reacted angrily to the criticism. He left the meeting in tears after being told by Welke and others that the method of introducing the idea to the public had been undemocratic.

That night, Steuart says, he seriously considered resigning. "I went home that night and said 'I've just had the worst day of my political life.' I thought the party was willing to let me retire gracefully but that day, I wondered if they didn't just want to get rid of me as quickly as possible."

Caucus colleague and longtime friend Cy MacDonald pulled him out of his thoughts of resignation. MacDonald called that night to tell Steuart he thought the episode had been an attempt by Lane and his supporters to force Steuart to resign so Lane could claim leadership. It gave Steuart a reason to fight back. The next day, he had a confrontation with Lane and told him he would make sure the leadership did not fall to Lane if "he didn't get off my back." Lane denied any ulterior motives, and in fact no one had declared himself a candidate yet. But the confrontation ended the issue and it did not surface again. Merchant had missed the Regina fireworks but he was called to Saskatoon later to an executive meeting and reprimanded.

However, while the actual controversy was short-lived, it left its scars. Despite the denials of most of those involved, many in the party continued to believe it was a plot by Lane to manipulate his way into the leadership. It also increased the long-standing antagonism between Steuart and Lane and made Steuart wary of anyone he felt had sided with Lane. It was the real beginning of the overt divisions which would plague the caucus and party during the next year. Steuart's ability to lead, even in the short term, had been damaged.

The race for the party presidency that fall proved to be equally divisive. It opened up the federal-provincial wounds which many in the party hoped would go away.

The fight for the presidency was launched when four-year veteran Garry Wilson announced he had had enough. During the fall, it became clear the issue would be federal-provincial relations and, in particular, division of the money collected through the federal tax credit system. With the election over, the provincial executive was anxious to have a permanent formula written for an annual division the money between the federal and provincial wings. Informally, the agreement remained a fifty/fifty split in off-election years and a seventy-five/twenty-five split in election years, but its informality still gave federal Liberals too much power to use the money as a bargaining lever.

One of the leaders of the "prov" position was director Terry Jenson of

Saskatoon, a businessman and popular executive member. Soon, he was being pressured to run for president on a platform of getting the division of money formalized. A campaign group began to form around him.

The opponent was Saskatoon lawyer Tom Molloy, Lang's 1974 campaign manager and a candidate considered by the Jenson group to be a "fed," in part because he would not agree with them that division of money was the most pressing issue. Molloy rejects the suggestion he was running as a candidate whose interest was to see the federal wing take control. "I thought the key requirement of the party was going to be organization and that was the area I've always been most interested in," he said later. "That's why I ran, not to be an Otto Lang man. But I wouldn't put forward a position on the funds until I knew the financial state of the party and they wouldn't tell me."

It was shaping up to be a classic fight. Lang, his wife Adrian, brother-in-law Merchant, and other Lang supporters considered in the "fed" camp were lined up on Molloy's side while the other side consisted of a collection of "provs" the like of which had not been seen for several years. But four weeks before the convention and leadership vote, Jenson disappeared along with three others during a charter flight from northern Manitoba to Saskatoon. No trace of the plane could be found (their bodies were discovered in the wreckage the next spring) and the Jenson camp was in a quandary. Should they find another candidate to oppose Molloy? With two weeks left before the December 5 vote, they decided to and approached former MLA Dr. Don Macdonald of Moose Jaw. He refused, and treasurer John Embury of Regina emerged as the candidate. The "prov" side quickly reorganized and, after a frantic two weeks, arrived at the Saskatoon convention site confident they had a chance.

The convention itself was the scene of intense campaigning as Embury supporters tried to sway delegates with arguments about the danger of a federal takeover of the party. When the vote was over, Embury had won and many of his supporters took it as a lesson to Lang and the "feds" that they weren't in control. Lang quickly began to dissociate himself from the Molloy campaign and attended a provincial executive meeting to disclaim involvement. Many skeptics remained unconvinced. "It gave Otto a message that he was a long way from controlling the Liberal Party in the province," according to Embury. He said later the leadership fight reopened many of the old fed-prov divisions, even though the money-sharing formula worked out soon after was virtually the same as that proposed by Jenson and Embury. Most of the presidential election intrigue went unnoticed by the media covering the convention, but the passions aroused were strong enough and the spectre of increasing divisions real enough that Lang was moved to warn provincial Liberals publicly not to use up energy fighting each other when there were more important political opponents to battle.

By this time, the Liberal party was divided, tired, and badly in need of a boost in spirit and morale. The NDP obliged.

The issue was the potash policies of the provincial government. On November 12, 1975, the first session of the new Legislature had opened with a government commitment to buy or take over a major portion of the provincial potash industry. It was the culmination of a long battle between the provincial government and the largely foreign-owned potash industry. It was a fight which often had left the Liberals caught in the middle of a complex drama in which there were no absolute rights and wrongs. The proposal for massive government expenditure to get into the mining industry was different. The Liberals knew that was wrong and they knew a majority of Saskatchewan people agreed with them at the time.

Although the dispute which culminated in the autumn of 1975 had started just a few years before, the potash industry had long been a political issue in the province. Through the years, the Liberals had been its friend, its supporter, and sometimes its critic.

For more than two decades, provincial politicians had held the industry out as the economic hope for the future. Potash is a major component of fertilizer, and as world population grows, the need for fertilizer to help feed the world's hungry grows as well. Potash was obviously a growth industry, and after deposits were first found in the 1940s and the first commercial mining venture was attempted in the early fifties, exploration was stepped up. It soon became apparent Saskatchewan was the site of one of the world's great potash reserves. The ruling CCF government of the day was not ignorant of the promises of development and jobs the deposits held. Talk of a future based on potash development became common, but except for one mine opening in 1951 and a second in 1958, the government of T. C. Douglas was not successful in beginning a great investment flood in the fifties. Both mines experienced water seepage and other technical problems which forced them to close, so when potash industry officials met Douglas in the early sixties, they held the upper hand. Tax concessions were offered to attract the industry, and investment started. International Minerals and Chemicals Corporation opened a mine in 1962, another was opened in 1964 by Kalium Chemicals, and the Potash Company of America reopened the mine which had closed in 1959.

By then, the Liberals were in power and the rush was on. Premier Thatcher encouraged American and Canadian companies to invest in the province, and in a well-publicized 1965 speech he made the potash industry the cutting edge in the fight against socialism. Cooperation between the industry and the government, he said, was "an experiment in private enterprise" which would be the acid test of his philosophy that opening the province to industrial development would create a better Saskatchewan. "It is our task to prove in the next few years that the private enterprise system can do more for our people than socialism."

Thatcher invited investment and it came in abundance. By the late 1960s, ten potash mines were operating in the province, providing thousands of jobs and an investment of hundreds of millions of dollars. But the dream soon began to sour. Potash markets became soft, prices fell to the point that companies were selling under the cost of production, and layoffs were imminent. In a desperate attempt to save his dream and the industry, Thatcher and New Mexico Governor David Cargo worked out a 1969 plan of production controls for the Saskatchewan industry which set a minimum price, saved some mines from closing, and at least kept the industry operating. It also averted United States tariff action against Canada, threatened because of charges that Canadian companies were dumping potash on the U.S. market and hurting the already staggering New Mexican industry.

Thatcher's plan was accompanied by some stern lectures from the premier who was outraged that the industry would overbuild and expose some of the flaws in the doctrine of unbridled corporate decision-making. The prorationing (production control) plan quickly became a hot political issue. While Thatcher defended the intervention into the industry as a necessary move, the Opposition NDP attacked it as a Liberal plan to prop up its "corporate friends." In the 1971 campaign, the potash industry became a prime example in the NDP attack on Liberal industrial policies, and the party promised to do away with prorationing, get more public benefits from the industry, and consider public ownership.

In office, the NDP soon found prorationing was working and the government quietly decided to let it continue working. But the government did move to raise more money from the industry — first by imposing a prorationing fee in 1972 and then by constructing a complex new tax system for the industry in 1974 which substantially raised tax revenue.[2] It also said the government wanted to acquire equity in the industry either through joint-venturing new mines with private companies or building its own mine near Yorkton. Throughout all this, the industry and its organization, Canadian Potash Producers Association, was digging in. It resisted the prorationing fee and Central Canada Potash Company took the government to court alleging the fee was unconstitutional. (This created a situation in which the provincial NDP government was defending in court a system of controls the party had once condemned as too pro-industry.) Other companies were fighting their own battle against the government. They refused to pay the prorationing fee and refused to open their books to the government, arguing the government was a potential competitor because it was planning a mine of its own. The stakes in the battle were high since the price of potash had soared, and the government stood to make more than $45 million a year from the new tax. The companies argued they were being taxed at an 80 percent rate and that they had just started to regain a portion of their investment after years of losing money.

It seemed like a situation perfect for the pro-industry Liberals. They had helped bring the industry into the province and could now argue the

---

[2] As early as 1972, the government began to receive reports, both internal and external, recommending a tougher stance and higher industry taxes, as well as the possibility of the government buying into the industry or building its own mine.

NDP was on the verge of driving it away. (The companies also began announcing cancellation of expansion plans, many of which had not been previously announced.) But the Liberals were wary of jumping too firmly on the industry bandwagon. The voters often tended to be skeptical of big companies, particularly companies with headquarters and profit bank accounts in the United States or Toronto. The result was a mixed Liberal position. They gleefully attacked the government for its "greed" and pointed to investment and potential jobs being lost, but they also were careful to say that in the face of increasing world prices, the industry had to be prepared to accommodate higher taxes on some of the windfall.

An uneasy lull fell over the dispute during the election campaign after an industry-government committee was established to look at the issues. On June 20, nine days after the NDP received a new mandate, industry spokesmen said they were suing the government over the reserves tax. They also would refuse to pay.

Within the government, all thought of resolving the issue peacefully ended. A select group of civil servants began to run down options available, and by fall NDP leaders had decided the government should take control of the industry through equity. While the Liberals were contenting themselves that summer with issuing occasional statements in favor of the right of the companies to take the government to court, NDP leaders were holding long, secret meetings to work out details of the biggest risk the Blakeney government would ever take. The basic decision had been to announce public acquisition of at least 50 percent of the productive capacity of the provincial potash industry. The mines would be acquired by purchase, although legislation would also give the government the power to expropriate if a sales agreement could not be worked out. A small group of civil servants, chosen from throughout the government for both their competence and their ideological commitment to the policy, formed a "potash task force" which spent long hours throughout the late summer and fall considering the options, preparing cost estimates, drawing up legislation, and preparing the announcement. The November 12, 1975, Throne Speech opening the new Legislature offered the public the first official word of the government plan "to acquire the assets of some or all of the producing potash mines in the province." Although the reaction of many was stunned silence while the implications of the move sank in, Steuart was quick off the mark with a condemnation. He had been tipped off beforehand and immediately issued a statement: "This is the greatest risk that has ever been launched by any provincial government."

Many uneasy voters in the province would have readily agreed with him. There were three major immediate questions: How much would it cost? Where would the money come from? What would be the reaction of the investment community and the private resource sector which provided tens of thousands of jobs?

There were no easy answers. Business and voter reaction would have to be judged on more than the immediate, off-the-cuff negative responses which started to be heard. The availability and cost of money to fund the purchases would not be known for months but government officials said the capital would be borrowed on international money markets and they were confident Saskatchewan's credit rating would result in a good deal. The question of cost would also have to wait, both for a government decision on how many mines to buy and on the results of negotiations between the companies and the government over price. However, there were estimates available and they received wide debate — total replacement value of the ten existing mines was estimated at $1.4 billion by government officials, and members of the potash task force had estimated the "fair market value" of the mines (the compensation principle contemplated by the legislation) at $1.3 billion.[3] Industry spokesmen claimed the assets were worth more than government estimates, but even accepting government figures and the pledge to acquire at least half the productive capacity, the bill would be a sizable $700 million. (By 1978, when the province had acquired 40 percent of the industry's productive capacity, it had invested more then $400 million, and late in the decade plans were announced to spend more than $1 billion more in a long-range upgrading and expansion program.)

The Liberal caucus quickly saw the potash policy as a chance to make good. Strategy meetings were held, industry officials were contacted, and a plan of action soon developed. The deal would be attacked on business, rather than ideological, grounds. The government would be questioned about money sources to be used for the purchase and attacked for risking taxpayer money when taxation powers could be used to extract high revenues if only the government would be more conciliatory with the industry.

As never before, Steuart came into his own as leader during those November days. He encouraged the MLAs to take stands, do research, and try to pin the government down. Although Ted Malone led the attack in the Legislature, Steuart was clearly in control. "Dave was excellent during those days," said one MLA who was normally a Steuart critic. "He led us, encouraged us to get involved, gave us inspiration."

Three things were working in the Liberals' favor in their campaign against the potash policy. The party had good contacts with the potash industry and received information to use in the steady stream of Liberal speeches, press conferences, and charges. At the same time, the Liberals had the floor to themselves. The seven PC MLAs under Dick Collver chose the curious tactic of remaining basically mute through the two-month debate which would follow. Collver argued the policy should be debated in the next election and any attempt to delay the legislation was a perversion of the legislative process. The Liberals were able to dominate media coverage

---

[3] John Richards and Larry Pratt, *Prairie Capitalism*. (Toronto: McClelland and Stewart, 1979), 270.

of the fight and ridicule the Tories at the same time. Finally, the enormity of the project and commitment of public funds had clearly stunned the electorate. The Liberals felt there was a large pool of fear and opposition to exploit and they did it well. Informal surveys, letters to the editor, radio phone-in shows, and trips to the country all confirmed they were leading a huge army of discontented, or at least frightened, people. Before the debate was over, even the NDP was conceding it probably didn't have majority support, but the policy was necessary and support would grow during the next three years when the benefits in jobs and revenue were seen.

By the time of the annual Liberal convention in Saskatoon, the party was riding a crest and the MLAs were looked upon almost as vanguard freedom fighters. Delegates took time out from their fighting over the next party president to support caucus efforts to fight the potash legislation. As the year ended, the caucus appeared united, morale was high, and the party was digging in for a long fight. The Legislature session had been carried into January as the Liberals refused to let the bills pass.

There was, of course, no chance that the legislation would be defeated, and by the time it was given final approval January 28, after more than forty days of debate and delaying tactics, the Liberals had won no major concessions or changes from the government. But they had kept Attorney-General Roy Romanow on the committee hotseat for days with often repetitive, but sometimes probing, questions, and that had shown the silent PCs up badly. Liberals had also given their self-image a boost and potential leadership candidates a chance to show their style. "In 40 days, we went from a bunch of greenhorns to a tight caucus," said an MLA. "Steuart did a magnificent job showing us the way. It was fun."

It was also not destined to last. When the session ended, the party tried to keep the issue and the momentum alive with a massive mail-out and questionnaire on the potash policy. Thousands were returned favoring the Liberals and they tried to score a propaganda victory from it, but the media were tired of the issue and success was limited. With the excitement wearing off, the problems of the party began to surface again. The organization had almost disappeared and many constituencies had not even bothered to have annual meetings the previous fall. Membership sales were down to a few thousand. Many looked to the impending leadership fight as a chance to revive the party, but already bitterness and divisions appeared to be creeping into the party around the camps of potential leadership candidates.

The Legislature session which opened March 12 did little to improve the situation. It went badly. Conservative leader Collver outshone Liberal questioners during debate on the provincial budget, Steuart seemed uninterested and ineffective, and Liberal efforts in the Legislature were uninspiring. MLA Colin Thatcher caused some embarrassment and bitterness with a March 30 speech attacking federal Liberals and the right to strike for civil servants. Steuart said later Thatcher's views did not represent the party, but the NDP saw it as a way to keep the federal-provincial split alive. In caucus, disputes and arguments were becoming more bitter as Steuart gave up control and rumored candidates Gary Lane, Ted Malone, Colin Thatcher, and Tony Merchant jockeyed for space and position.

As the session ended May 9, the caucus and party appeared to be spinning aimlessly. Lane and Malone were preparing to begin cross-province treks to test party support for their candidacies. Steuart was contemplating the Senate and trying to decide the best time to announce his resignation officially so the sparring for a replacement could begin in earnest, and in public.

Chapter Eleven

IN SEARCH OF A LEADER

On December 11, 1976, in a smoky, hot convention hall at the Centre of the Arts in Regina, the era of Dave Steuart in the Saskatchewan Liberal party ended. Over 1,100 Liberals had gathered to elect a successor to Steuart and, although they paid tribute to the efforts of their spent leader, he no longer figured in the frantic politicking which overtakes a political party at such turning points. Steuart had vowed not to play the role of kingmaker by favoring a candidate, and to the average delegate he remained true to his word. In official speeches and corridor encounters, they praised him, but his role there was that of an instant statesman, not a key player.

After more than two decades of steady politicking, Steuart seemed to enjoy his new-found status. The tributes were payment for his years of effort and he savored the sensation. Prime Minister Pierre Trudeau had considerably improved the occasion two days earlier when he announced Steuart had been appointed to the Senate. With no more elections to win and recognition from the most powerful Liberal in the country, Steuart could afford to enjoy himself. The Senate appointment was something he had actively sought, but the reality was no less an honor in his mind.[1] But while delegates and party officials told him they were pleased with the appointment, they were more interested in getting the convention over and installing a new leader. It had been a long, tiring, and sometimes demoralizing campaign which they wanted to end.

The campaign for a new leader had unofficially started more than a year earlier when Steuart made it plain after the election that he would not take the party into another one. Potential candidates began considering the

---

[1] After making his first contact with Lang about a Senate seat in 1975, he followed it with similar expressions of interest to Senator Keith Davey and Prime Minister Trudeau in 1976. By fall, he knew he was being considered, and Lang supported a Steuart appointment.

possibility of running, and testing the waters of party support and financial backing. The behind-the-scenes campaigning gathered strength throughout the winter and began to take its toll in party unity and discipline. By June, Steuart realized he would have to announce formally his decision to resign and call a leadership convention.

He chose to do it June 12 at a party fund-raising dinner in Regina. He told the crowd, which paid out over $150,000 to the Liberal party that night, that a leadership convention would be called for December 11 and he hoped candidates would travel the province looking for support and selling the message of the party. "There's nothing that will revitalize the Liberal party more than these two events," he told the crowd. But he added a warning as well. "Let's not kid ourselves. Let's not be under any delusions. We're at a crossroads in the Liberal Party. We've got a third party now and it's there. You can't ignore it."

Steuart later told an interviewer he had decided to announce his official resignation date then because "it's much nicer to walk away from something than to be pushed away." He left the leadership candidates a full six months to campaign, he said, because it would be more time to enthuse the party and because he expected a number of candidates to enter the race and the extra time would give them all a chance to become known. The decision to make the campaign so long would later be regretted by the candidates, many in the party, and even Steuart. As the campaign wore on and the policy issues had been debated, personality attacks and bitter personal rivalries became more divisive than envigorating.

The race got off to a fast start. Shortly after Steuart had made it official, three candidates plunged in and there were rumors of many more waiting for the right moment. The first candidates to stand up were three Regina lawyers — Malone, Merchant, and Lane. Within that trio were the makings of an interesting and vigorous fight. Merchant, as a brother-in-law of Lang, was considered the "fed." Lane, as a former Thatcher-government aide, was considered the "prov," and Malone, although once identified with the Lang lawyer brigades in the province, was considered the middle ground. Despite their similarity of profession, they represented enough ideological and loyalty diversity to offer a clear choice. An added ingredient early in the race was the bitterness some Malone workers felt toward the Merchant camp because Merchant had at one time disavowed any intention of running and had pledged himself to work for Malone. He had in fact advised Malone on tactics and policy for a while, and some Malone supporters thought this gave him an inside track on knowing what the Malone campaign would be like.

The campaign was just two weeks old when the original scenerio began to break down. Despite some support in caucus and on the party executive, Lane announced June 25 he would be withdrawing from the race. It was an unexpected move and Lane refused to clarify his reasons. He said he would have more to say later and then dropped out of sight. His opponents in the party quickly attributed his departure to their belief that Lane would not have won the leadership. However, since Lane had a following, a reputation as an organizer, and five months before the convention, that explanation did not seem entirely credible. It would be almost three months before Lane surfaced again to explain his moves and to express discontent with the Liberal party, but within days of his June announcement, he was telling friends and supporters he had quit because he felt the "fed" side of the party was uniting against him and he could not beat it. He said he was getting out of the race because he felt the provincial party was becoming increasingly dominated by the federal wing and he felt he could not have coped with the trend as leader.

As part of his evidence of a federal campaign against him, including Steuart, Lane told friends Steuart had called a special caucus meeting June 25 to change the date of the leadership convention to help either Malone or Merchant. Steuart denies it and there is no direct evidence, but the caucus call was curious. Notices of a "very important caucus" to discuss "the timing of the leadership convention and other matters vital to the party" were sent to MLAs June 20. Yet when MLAs assembled, they had little to discuss and Steuart made no proposals other than that it be at the regular Liberal convention, as he had already announced. The only major event between June 20 and the caucus meeting was Lane's announcement that he was pulling out. Later, Steuart said the caucus had been called merely to confirm the schedule, but that does not adequately explain the implied importance in the caucus notice.

MLA Sonny Anderson was an early Lane supporter who had turned down a proposal to work for Merchant so he could be free to work for Lane. When he heard the Lane announcement on radio, he called. "Gary told me he couldn't beat the Lang-Merchant team," Anderson said. "I asked him if he was supporting either of the other two and he said he wasn't. We were free to do what we wanted." Merchant soon called again and this time Anderson agreed to act as his campaign manager in charge of organizing (even though he remained convinced Lane would have won if he had stayed in the race).

At that point, there were still hopes within the party that other candidates would come forward to join Merchant and Malone. President John Embury, MLAs Stuart Cameron, Jack Wiebe, Glen Penner, and Colin Thatcher, and MP Cliff McIsaac were all rumored as possible candidates. Many in the party felt the two Regina lawyers, long-time friends and identifiable Lang supporters, did not offer delegates enough choice. Some, like MLA Linda Clifford, spent weeks talking to prospective candidates, trying to convince them to jump in because neither Malone nor Merchant were attractive enough candidates to keep the party strong and widely popular.

In the end, none would make the commitment. Many mused in public that they were being pressured because neither existing candidate seemed totally acceptable. Then they too decided not to run. The last chance came in early November when within days, Embury, Cameron, Thatcher, and

Saskatoon businessman Gerry Fraser publicly speculated and then declined. The whole process made the party look bad. Instead of being read as a sign that many were interested in the job, it became interpreted in the media as a sign of weakness when so many saw the existing candidates as inadequate, yet didn't want to throw themselves into the struggle. It brought to mind an April column by Allan Fotheringham in *Maclean's Magazine:* "The Liberals planned a leadership convention this year to relieve little Davey Steuart of the weary mantle but things are so bad they may have to cancel the immolation ceremony because a new kamikaze candidate has yet to offer himself for the sacrifice."

Malone was a thirty-nine-year-old who carried around as baggage the image, attitudes, and instincts of Regina's cloistered upper class. He was a member of a well-established family (an ORF in Regina jargon — old Regina family) and his power base was the well-to-do Regina Lakeview area of stately homes, tree-lined streets, and upper level professionals. His maternal grandfather James Grassick had served as Regina mayor and was a Conservative in the thirties provincial cabinet of J.T.M. Anderson. Malone's father was a backroom Liberal who managed a brewery and lived in affluence in Depression-era Regina. Malone's early life included maids and the symbols of wealth. He had graduated from the University of Saskatchewan with a law degree in 1962 when Lang was the dean of law. He quickly became one of the Regina lawyers chosen by Lang to organize federal ridings when federal and provincial parties were not on speaking terms. That made him suspect to the provincial leadership at the time but he also became involved in provincial politics by working as campaign manager for Regina Lakeview MLA Don McPherson in 1967 and 1971. He was constituency president for a while and served on the provincial executive. Still, because of his identification with Lang, Malone was generally considered a "fed." In 1973 when McPherson died, Malone won the nomination in a tough battle against four others and went on to win Regina Lakeview in a by-election with a larger majority than McPherson had won. In the Legislature for three years, he projected an image of thoughtful moderation and did a credible job leading the Liberal party's battle against the 1975 potash legislation. However, he also had some liabilities in the party. He had a reputation for lacking imagination, being a chauvinist, and lacking drive. With his frequent cigar and tendency to use formal, courtroom language in political speeches, he often appeared to be the epitome of the lawyer in politics. Clearly, Malone was the establishment figure and his campaign planners hoped to make him appear more of a populist with a feel for average voter concerns.

Merchant was a thirty-one-year-old lawyer with his roots deeply set in Saskatchewan Liberal politics. However, his personal credentials as a provincial Liberal were viewed by some as shaky, and he began the race with some clear liabilities. He grew up in Saskatoon, the grandson of a Yorkton judge and son of Sally Merchant, a Liberal MLA of the sixties. Sister Adrian had married then Dean of Law and federal Liberal mover Otto

Lang in 1963, and Merchant's major interest had always seemed to be federal. His career as a Regina lawyer had been successful but his approach to law and the politics of the Saskatchewan bar had led him into some run-ins with the Law Society of Saskatchewan, including several publicly-announced reprimands from the organization for breaches of association ethics.[2] However, he proved to be a popular candidate in the 1975 election, recording the second highest victory margin (1,374 votes) among all the Liberal winners. During his year and a half in the Legislature, Merchant was one of the hardest-working members of caucus. He offered more private member's bills than any other MLA, made well-researched speeches on a variety of topics, and offered often intelligent and well-backgrounded criticism of government labor and women's rights records. From his experience working in the media, he had a well-honed sense of how to manipulate reporters to get news coverage, and he quickly developed a reputation as an MLA who worked his riding well, using voters' lists, mail-outs, and canvasses to keep his name known and his image positive. Within the party, his image was that of a hard-working, competent politician with too-strong family connections to the federal Liberals and an ambition which combined with a disturbing lack of scruples when it came to playing the game of getting ahead. Anderson says when he became campaign manager, planners saw several obstacles they would have to overcome to sell Merchant — his Lang connection, his reputation for having an unorthodox style, and his image as a manipulator. "Tony is a hard commodity to sell," Anderson said later.

The decision was made by the Merchant planners to try to sell their candidate as the one who would shake the party up, head it in a new direction, and undo the mistakes of the past. They would concentrate on the young and discontented and leave to Malone the section of the party which was comfortable, in control, and appalled at any thought of a radical change in direction or approach. Malone, on the other hand, was content to campaign for some change in policy and style, and a return to basic liberal principles rather than the antisocialism of the Steuart and Thatcher years. But he was offering continuity — a change in emphasis, not direction.

Merchant dropped his first bombshell on July 31. He flew to a series of news conferences around the province to announce he believed the federal and provincial sections of the party should formally split into separate constitutional organizations. He argued it would leave the provincial party freer to battle provincial issues and it would attract more votes by freeing the provincial party from the hostility Saskatchewan voters felt for the federal government. "It's really designed to make supporters of the

---

[2] The two incidents drawing official reprimands were contacting another lawyer's client directly, rather than through counsel, and dispensing legal advice over Regina Radio CJME. Although members of the lawyers' society say other complaints were filed about Merchant, none had been dealt with and settled.

provincial party who are nervous about the union with the federal party more comfortable," he said.

It was an unexpected move and, because of his federal ties, there was some skepticism that he meant it. The proposal was widely viewed as an antifederal stance by Merchant, although that was not necessarily so. Implementation of the policy would clearly have freed the provincial party of some of the obligations to defend federal policy, but by creating a separate and equal federal wing, it would also have been institutionalizing the power of Lang and his supporters. Since fund-raising initiative had been flowing to the federal level, the federal division still would have had substantial power over the provincial wing, but provincial Liberals would no longer have had any semblance of control over federal party activities in the province. At best, the proposal would have been a mixed blessing for provincial Liberals worried about federal ties.

However, the public perception was that it was an attack on federal Liberals, and Merchant campaign manager Sonny Anderson said it was a policy created and enunciated in part as a political gamble to try to counter the hostility because of the candidate's Lang connection. In a way, it worked because Malone quickly came out against the Merchant proposal and aligned himself clearly with the federal camp. "I'm seeking the leadership of the Liberal Party not to divide it but to unite it," he said. "I think it is most unfortunate that this suggestion has been made at this time." Many others in the party agreed, hoping the issue which had plagued the party for decades would go away. However, once it had been raised, the media, delegates, and Merchant would not let it go away. The debate over the troubling topic of federal-provincial relations played a role throughout the campaign. It was a gamble by Merchant which probably won him some support among fringe Liberals and the old anti-fed camp. It also undoubtedly convinced many of the swing delegates that Merchant was not the man for the job.

In the next five months, the two candidates travelled thousands of miles to attend constituency annual meetings where delegates to the convention were chosen. They spent hours trying to sway the 1,500 Liberals who would be eligible to vote. The campaign ended with a series of joint meetings across the province where the candidates outlined their views and fielded questions.

Some natural policy differences developed during this time as the candidates outlined their respective plans for a Liberal reawakening. Merchant promised to sell back to the private sector the government-owned resource industries if he were elected premier. Malone doubted if the private sector would take the risk of buying them back and suggested instead creation of an Alberta-inspired public resource company in which individuals could buy shares. Merchant promised a decentralization of the party, a greater role for the membership in making policy, and a move for himself from Regina to Saskatoon where he promised to take on personally a provincial cabinet minister in his own seat in the next election. Malone made no offer to move out of Regina and he insisted the caucus should continue to play the leading role in policy making. He did propose a decentralization of organization and structure, however.

Malone offered the most detailed policy proposals. Near the end of the campaign, he issued a series of policy papers which dealt with areas ranging from health care (a streamlining of health costs, more emphasis on acute care hospital facilities, and reintroduction of utilization fees if necessary to pay for it) to labor relations (creation of a public overseer who would sit in on labor negotiations affecting the public and have the power to order a change in negotiators or a cooling-off period in an effort to avert a threatened strike).

These policy differences were expected and encouraged by party members. It gave them a choice and showed the party had a range of options open to it. However, the two candidates and their supporters also engaged in some mudslinging and bickering over some very sensitive party issues which did little for Liberal credibility or image in the eyes of the public.

One of the issues was the way in which delegate support was being gathered.

During the campaign, the media carried a series of stories indicating the Merchant camp, and to a lesser extent Malone, were using the slate system at constituency meetings. Basically, each candidate would circulate a list of potential delegates who would support him for leader. Members supporting the same candidate were supposed to vote for the delegate slate. It was a tactic used by countless politicians in previous campaigns (including the 1971 Liberal leadership campaign) but this time reporters jumped on the issue and ran stories quoting Liberal, Conservative, and NDP officials saying the slate system was undemocratic. One of the real problems was that uncommitted longtime Liberal members were being excluded from the convention because they were not on a slate and this caused some internal grumbling. Many Merchant slate members were young, first-time Liberals and that led to charges of "twenty-four-hour Liberals" who showed up for the constituency meeting, won election, and then left without taking an interest in the party.[3]

It was a case of normal political backrooming being exposed to the public. The party, rather than treating it as such and downplaying the issue, let it get out of hand. Party officials, including President Embury, criticized the Merchant camp, and Malone made an issue of publicly announcing the slate system was undemocratic and that he would not use it again. He

---

[3] Two separate incidents illustrate the discontent Merchant's tactics were causing in the party. In Regina, Merchant workers paid the entrance fee to a constituency meeting for some young potential delegates, and there were charges of bribery. In Saskatoon, after the Merchant slate was elected at one meeting, a straw vote showed Malone the favorite. Merchant supporters had already left while Malone supporters stayed to hear the speeches.

challenged Merchant to do the same, and the implication was left that if the practice did not stop, the entire process of choosing a leader would be suspect. In the Merchant camp, the slate system was considered politics-as-usual and there was no intention of changing. Campaign manager Anderson said he was largely responsible for implementing it, and as a way to win the convention, he also developed a plan to have Merchant delegates bussed to the December convention and billeted in private homes to save expenses. "We were getting the younger delegates who didn't have the money to come to Regina for two or three days at their own expense. Call it bribery if you will, but we thought it unfair that they couldn't play as much of a role as Malone's affluent supporters," said an organizer. Merchant planners felt the critics of their tactics were being hypocritical, since it had been done before. The difference, said Anderson, was that someone in the Merchant group liked to talk to the press. "As soon as I'd propose these things, they'd be leaked to the press and someone would be down our neck," he said. "We got bad press over it and a bad image. But as a guy who likes to deal with numbers, I think it was the way to go."

The public feuding and charges of a lack of democracy and bribery did little to help the party image.

However the most damaging issue to haunt the leadership candidates as they roamed the province was the Progressive Conservative party and how Liberals should react to it. Steuart had started the campaign by warning that they could not afford to ignore the Tories and that was never more clear than during 1976 when the Liberal organization all but collapsed while the PCs were working hard, building constituency organizations, selling memberships, and watching the Liberals cut one another up. Then on October 25, Gary Lane announced he was leaving the Liberal caucus to become a PC because the Liberals "no longer reflect the feelings of Saskatchewan people." He said they had sold out to the federal Liberals at the expense of their commitments to the province. Liberals quickly reacted to the defection by claiming Lane had left because he knew he couldn't become Liberal leader. Beneath the surface, though, the Lane move was troubling. Many in the party were genuinely glad to see him go, feeling he had been a negative influence in the caucus. Others saw him as a skillful politician with a solid constituency within the party and outside it. In addition to drawing the numbers of Liberals and Conservatives in the Legislature closer together, Lane's conversion was an important boost for the Tories because it gave them their first real urban seat and an MLA with five years' experience in the House.

It became a minor topic of conversation at subsequent Liberal leadership meetings but three weeks later, Merchant made the Tories a major issue. He told a forum in Saskatoon that if elected leader, he would be willing to talk with the PCs to see what could be done to "elect more private initiative people." He said he did not favor joint candidates between the two parties, but he thought some cooperation might be in order. If elected premier with a minority government, he said, he would offer the

PCs some seats in the cabinet. It was another good issue for Malone. He quickly said he would not follow the same route. "When you boil it down, what do you have? You have a deal with the Tories." It was another issue neither the media nor the delegates would let drop and for the next three weeks, Liberal party officials cringed over the prospect of the two leadership candidates publicly debating what accommodation they could make with the surging Tories.

When delegates began arriving for the convention December 9, many party officials were privately predicting a close vote with a likely Merchant victory. President Embury said later he felt Merchant had had a "comfortable lead" in early November, but some of the tactics and bad publicity after that had eroded it. Anderson says during the month before the convention, Merchant planners felt they had "a cushion of 50 or 60 votes." Merchant himself was energetic and friendly at the convention. Malone looked tired and appeared testy when confronted with anyone not clearly a supporter.

The first major sign of trouble for the Merchant forces came when few of the younger delegates elected on slates outside Regina appeared to be arriving at the convention centre. By the morning of the vote, it was becoming clear the gamble had failed. Close to 400 elected delegates had not appeared and it seemed many were the young "twenty-four-hour Liberals" the party establishment had so disdained. Anderson blamed it on the fact that his idea for bussing the delegates in and billeting them had never been organized. "We did a hell of a job of getting delegates elected," he said. "But we didn't have a good delivery system The votes were there. I just didn't get them out."

He complained that as the campaign progressed, the image makers began to take precedence over the organizers as media ads and promotion gimmicks began to absorb more attention and money than practical problems of getting the vote out. The final mistake was the last candidate appearance before the delegates on the afternoon of December 11, minutes before the vote. Malone stood with his family nearby and gave a traditional, solid speech about the strength of the party and better days ahead. Merchant chose the slick route with a multimedia presentation, balloons, and a band with his own theme song. If there were any uncommitted left in the hall largely filled with representatives of the conservative middle class, it was the wrong approach to win their votes. "It was a perfect Ontario campaign," Merchant said later, "But it didn't sell in Saskatchewan."

The vote confirmed it. Malone, 628, Merchant, 521. Almost 400 eligible delegates had not voted. In the crush of excitement which followed, Malone told delegates it was not the end of a long campaign but just the beginning, working toward the 1979 election. In the confusion on stage, the usual ritual of having the defeated candidates ask that the result be made unanimous was not performed. Was it a mistake or a promise of divisions to come? Many Merchant supporters felt President Embury had deliberately tried to embarrass Merchant by not offering him the microphone to call for unity. Embury said Merchant had made no move and he did not feel it his obligation to seek Merchant out. Either way, it was not a good omen.

That evening, Malone delegates partied and savored the victory of middle-of-the-roadism and continuity over unorthodoxy and uncertainty. A band of several hundred Merchant supporters huddled in several rooms at the Regina Inn, many in tears and many bitterly complaining about the "establishment" ganging up on their candidate. Merchant sat on the floor in a crowded room, watching a television set and feeling the crush of sympathizers. He told reporters he would stay in the party and work with Malone: "We've been friends all our lives." But he couldn't promise anything about his supporters. "Many of the people who supported me were committed to me and the change we would make to the party," he said. "That support may not be transferrable."

At thirty-nine, Ted Malone had won the leadership of the Saskatchewan Liberal party. But what had he inherited? Was it a prize worth the eight-month battle? In the flush of victory, the answer was an obvious yes. The challenges of the months ahead would provide a less emotional basis for deciding.

Chapter Twelve

THE MALONE YEARS

Ted Malone began his tenure as Liberal leader without the euphoria normally associated with political triumphs. "I felt nothing but relief, no joy," he said later of the moment when the convention results were announced. "I just sagged and said 'Thank God it's over.' "

It was an appropriately sombre reaction from the new leader, considering the task which lay ahead. Even a superficial analysis of the party at the time showed it in a troubled state. The divisions of the leadership race were very evident and reports from the countryside indicated that while the Liberal organization turned its energies to the leadership race, the Conservatives had been filling in the vacuum. Many Liberal riding associations had become dormant and a sense of defeatism had invaded party ranks in the face of the Tory surge. The party was also tired after eight months of steady politicking in search of a leader. Members and workers seemed more anxious to go back to their private lives and to take a few months off from politics than to begin an assault on the Conservatives to win back lost ground. "We were flat," President John Embury said.

Malone says it took him little time to realize the seriousness of the situation. Based on the enthusiasm of the leadership campaign, he had assumed he was inheriting a broadly-based, strong organization. Instead, he found a shell. "The tip was there, the enthusiastic leaders," he said. "But that was all. The iceberg underneath had melted."

Within days of the convention, several incidents made the problems all the more obvious. On December 12, he met retiring leader Senator Steuart to talk about the party and the by-election which would have to be called to fill the vacant Prince Albert-Duck Lake seat Steuart had held. "I talked to Dave and I saw immediately there was nobody to run in Prince Albert," Malone said later. The party organization in the riding was weak, and with

Steuart gone as a candidate, it would be a hard fight. "I realized we were in big trouble," said the new leader.

The same day, Malone accidentally met Merchant in the area of Regina where they both live. It was not a pleasant meeting and Merchant showed some bitterness about the convention outcome, which was unsettling for Malone. Several days later, it became worse when Lang paid a visit. "Otto came and screamed at me because Tony hadn't spoken after the vote was announced at the convention," Malone said later. "It was not our doing. We were flabbergasted. That was the cause of immediate bitterness."

With those portents to consider and the party obviously on the slide, Malone had some clear challenges to face. He had to unite the party, rebuild the organization on an almost riding-by-riding basis, and reverse the defeatism. He had to convince antigovernment voters in the province that the Liberals were an alternative to the NDP and a better alternative than the Conservatives. He had to put his own stamp on the party and, through that, interest and excite the province.

At the best of times, it would be a tall order. In January 1977, it was simply next-year country. The immediate task facing the Liberals was to fight two by-elections which were no-win situations. They were being held March 2 in Prince Albert-Duck Lake and Saskatoon Sutherland to fill vacancies in seats formerly held by Liberals. Prince Albert had been Senator Steuart's seat since 1962, but with small-margin wins in most campaigns, it could not be considered safe Liberal territory. The Saskatoon seat was a new constituency first contested in 1975 and it had been won by popular former alderwoman Evelyn Edwards, who died in autumn 1976. The best the Liberals could do was win both and maintain the status quo. A loss in either riding would be another indication of decline and could speed up the process.

The party strategy for those two crucial votes has been a matter of controversy within Liberal circles. On January 14, two weeks before the vote was actually announced, Malone made it clear the stakes were high. If Liberals win both, he told reporters, "we can legitimately say we have pricked the Tory bubble." By implication, a loss would confirm that the Liberals were on the decline.

By mid-January, all parties had nominated candidates in the two ridings and the race was on. Duck Lake Mayor Alex Baribeau was the Liberal candidate in Prince Albert, and businessman Gerry Fraser was the Saskatoon candidate. The issues were the usual Saskatchewan election fare — debate over government resource policies, Opposition promises to operate the health care system better and to reduce the size of government and the tax load. But for the Liberals, the issue was more fundamental. The new leader and the strength of the party were on the line.

The party began the fights with several disadvantages. While the leadership race had been on, the PCs had been working the ridings, nominating their candidates, and laying the groundwork. Liberal organizations in the two ridings were not strong and both had been pro-Merchant in the leadership vote. In a sense, Malone was walking into enemy territory when he dropped into the Liberal organizations for the campaigns.

From the beginning, the Liberals appeared to be just minor actors in the by-elections. The focus was on the PCs and their obvious momentum. Tory candidates capitalized on that by waging high-profile campaigns, attacking provincial government health care and resource policies, and tying provincial Liberals to unpopular federal Liberal policies. The provincial New Democrats ran defensive campaigns. Voters were still uncertain over the government's resource policies, and while more than $100 million had been invested to buy potash facilities, no obvious benefits were in evidence yet. The opposition and the media had also been battering the government with allegations that tight money policies and wrong spending priorities were hurting the health care system. Although NDP candidates denied the charges, they spent much of their time answering accusations. The Liberals were left out in these rhetorical battles. Although they tried to score with their own attacks on both government policy and Conservative performance, they most often found themselves facing charges of irrelevance. In both ridings, the organizations were scrambling, the momentum seemed to be with the Conservatives, and Liberal policies were either ill-defined or nonexistent. Malone had not been party leader long enough to have left a mark on the party image, and in the almost two years since the general election defeat, the Liberal party had done little to re-establish itself in the public mind as a credible alternative with attractive policies. Mid-term by-elections often become a chance for voters to reprimand the government without danger that it will fall. The Liberal challenge in Prince Albert and Saskatoon was to convince voters it was a more logical repository for such antigovernment sentiments than the PCs.

Much of the burden fell on the new leader Malone, and in the aftermath of the vote, there were two party views of his role. Merchant, who quickly became a consistent behind-the-back critic of Malone, argues he did not get working in the new ridings early enough and did not mobilize the full forces of the party well enough. "In both by-elections, it was as though Ted did not realize that defeat would destroy the Liberal party," he said later. The other view is that Malone did too much. He worked full time during the last month before the vote, knocking on doors, trying to sell himself and the candidates. Some party officials later said that was a mistake. "We sat down and thought we might as well take advantage of Ted as a new leader," said President Embury. "We did that and it was a mistake." On election night, the PCs won both ridings from the Liberals. In Prince Albert, Baribeau placed third. In Saskatoon, Fraser ran second by more than 500 votes.

The results were a startling indication of growing Tory strength in urban areas and the dissatisfaction voters were feeling with both government policy and Liberal alternatives. In Prince Albert, Garnet Wipf was able to pick up some of the organization and support which had sent John Diefenbaker to Parliament for twenty-five years. The PCs were also able to capitalize on some community unease over the situation at the Prince Albert Penitentiary by taking a strong law-and-order stand. The vote also showed that much of the traditional provincial Liberal support in the city had been personal support for Steuart.

In Saskatoon, Tory Harold Lane attracted support from both traditional Liberal and NDP areas of the riding. Middle-class voters in the Cumberland and Grosvenor areas of the city switched emphatically from Liberal to PC. Traditional working-class, union areas of Sutherland switched from the NDP to the PCs, hurting Liberal chances for a slim victory up the middle. Personalities, a strong Tory pitch for law and order, and promises of more local control and a switch in resource policies had a strong impact. NDP candidate Anne Boulton campaigned heavily on the government's move into the potash industry. Voters were still wary of the move and not willing to endorse it.

Election night was a disaster for the Liberals. Malone had put his credibility and reputation on the line and lost. The Conservative momentum, in Malone's own words, gathered force. Even worse, Liberal organizations in other areas of the province had deteriorated more as all party efforts for the past two months had been concentrated on the by-elections.

Steuart immediately blamed the losses on federal policies. Malone said voters had been opposing both federal and provincial governments by voting Tory, so it was not a reflection of their views on provincial Liberals. "This was only a skirmish. The major battle has yet to be fought," he told disheartened workers on election night. Privately, party leaders were alarmed. They felt they had made a tactical error by putting so much emphasis on Malone when there was a chance it might backfire. "We knew going into the by-elections they probably couldn't be won," said Embury. "We shouldn't have hung them on Ted." Some party officials were also concerned about some features of the new leader which surfaced during the by-election campaigns. In Saskatoon Sutherland, for example, he had alienated some female workers by issuing orders, expecting them to fetch coffee and look after his whims when he was in the office. Considering that many from the organization had supported Merchant for leader, it was not the right time to try to exercise some of the perks of leadership.

Five days after the by-elections, the Legislature opened and the two new PCs were sworn in. Liberals held just two seats more than the Tories now, twelve to ten, and with by-election-night predictions of Liberal demise ringing in their ears, the spotlight was on the Liberal caucus.

During the session, Liberals showed themselves again to be the most effective Opposition MLAs. After the $1.51 billion budget was introduced, Malone and the newly-appointed finance critic Colin Thatcher hammered the NDP over big government, deficits, and tax increases when economic times in the province were good. Liberals defended private enterprise in mining when the government introduced a bill to establish the Saskatchewan Mining Development Corporation, a Crown company. They called for better treatment for the province's native people, and labor critic Merchant proposed some pro-union changes to labor laws.

Despite their good showing, however, the Liberals found themselves unable to compete with the PCs for headlines or government attention. The PCs won wide media coverage with Legislature charges about brutality at some northern wilderness camps and the declining quality of hospital conditions because of government restraint in health spending. In both cases, Tory charges were less than accurate, but they got the all-important media coverage. They also drew the wrath of government speakers and that contributed to the image of the PCs as the real Opposition. It was a pattern which began to appear during the by-election campaigns and was to continue for the next year. The NDP carried it to the extreme in the Legislature when Continuing Education Minister Dr. Don Faris, a United Church minister, accused the PCs of offering bigotry and dishonesty "masquerading under the holy name of religion." He tried to paint the 1977 version of the PCs as direct descendants of the Anderson government of the 1930s, which had included support from the Ku Klux Klan. "Not since the Ku Klux Klan-Conservative alliance of 1929 have the Saskatchewan people seen such a combination of bigotry and religion for political purposes," he said. And rarely had the people of Saskatchewan seen political debate reduced to that sleazy level. Faris's charges gave the PCs reason to protest and kept the spotlight on them. The Liberals could do little to compete. "The NDP created the Tory monster," Malone was later to complain bitterly. It was an exaggeration with at least an element of truth in it.

The Legislature sitting led directly into a by-election campaign to fill a vacancy created by the death of NDP member Leonard Larson. The June 8 vote in Pelly was officially a test of government strength, since it had been an NDP stronghold and the riding, in the east-central portion of the province, contained more state-owned land-bank land than any other constituency. The government record and farm policies were major issues. But again, as far as the Liberals were concerned, it was a test of their strength against the Conservatives. The real race was for second place, and both Opposition parties threw all they had into the campaign. MLA Neil McMillan became a full-time organizer, Malone and several other MLAs virtually moved to the riding for the month, and such federal Liberal luminaries as recently converted former-PC Jack Horner and Indian Affairs and Northern Development Minister Warren Allmand visited. The Liberals spent over $30,000 — more than three times the legally allowed amount under provincial law, but again it was to no avail. Election night was another disaster. The NDP won as expected, but the Conservative candidate placed second and the Liberals' Donn Walsh placed third. In 1975, the PCs had lost their deposit and the Liberals won 32 percent of the vote — the provincial average. In the by-election, the PCs increased to 29 percent and the Liberals dropped to 21 percent.

For Malone, it was another night of excuses and worry. "Liberals are going to have to decide whether they are going to be Liberals or not in the years ahead," he told supporters. It was his first official indication that the struggle was not for government or even second place, but for survival.

The by-election defeat brought the beginning of a series of strange NDP attempts to prop up Liberal morale. NDP leaders were beginning to worry that a complete Liberal collapse would solidify the antigovernment majority under one umbrella and that would be bad news. The answer was to try to make the Liberals look more credible, and a series of NDP back-handed defences of Liberal chances seemed aimed at doing just that. When PC leader Collver predicted the by-election represented one more step in the "demise" of the Liberals, Premier Blakeney responded: "I think the political life of Canada is strewn with the corpses of people who had written off the Liberal Party." He predicted better days ahead for Liberals because the federal party appeared to be gaining strength in the province. For many Liberals, such words of encouragement from an old enemy were simply rubbing salt in the wounds.

Malone immediately had other problems to counter. June featured a series of demoralizing news stories as various members of the Liberal caucus speculated publicly about leaving the party. Tony Merchant and Stuart Cameron said they were considering running in the next federal election. Jack Wiebe was also considering a move to federal politics but after the Pelly defeat, he said he was reconsidering because the provincial party needed help. Colin Thatcher was speculating about leaving the Liberal party altogether and rumors were that he was negotiating with the PCs. Malone clearly had to act to save face. He called a caucus session June 15 and for five hours listened to complaints; then he laid down the law that there was to be no more public speculating about leaving the party. Nine days later, Thatcher left to join the PCs. The Legislature opposition parties were now tied in seats at eleven. The Liberals lost the right to claim official Opposition status and Malone lost $4,294 a year in salary.

Liberal leaders reacted quickly and bitterly to Thatcher's defection. "I invite all the rest of the opportunists to join Colin and the Conservatives now," said President Embury. They said they were glad to see him go because he had been a disruptive factor and a political lightweight. But the Thatcher move was more important than they were willing to admit and more complex than they painted it. As the son of former Liberal Premier Thatcher, Colin's presence in provincial politics carried some symbolic significance. He was primarily a right-wing antisocialist, rather than a philosophic Liberal. He had made it clear for months that his interest was in defeating the NDP and he would join any group which appeared able to do that. Like his father, he was anti-federal Liberal and during the Pelly by-election, he refused to work because federal Liberals were involved. Thatcher was a tall, quick-tempered straight-talking rancher who saw himself as strong and admired strength in others. After he bolted the party, he told friends the final straw with the Liberals had been kind NDP words about them in their hour of weakness and the fact that Malone had not been more firm with him in caucus. "If Ted had laid down the line, I might have stayed," he said. "Instead, he tried to avoid a confrontation. I decided then to leave." It is unlikely he would have stayed in any circumstance, but clearly the issue was more complex than the Liberals painted it. Thatcher was an opportunist interested in teaming up with winners, but his dissatisfaction was also a warning sign that the Malone Liberals were less than satisfactory to the traditional anti-NDP, anti-Ottawa Liberals. His leaving was an important symbolic blow to the Liberals.

For the next few months, the party appeared to go underground. Its image slipped from public view. Behind the scenes, though, things were still going wrong. After the Pelly by-election, several high-priced organizers were hired to begin the organizational rebuilding but they proved costly and ineffective. The party organization lacked direction after former Executive Director Barb McNiven left to work with the Alberta Liberal party and no one was hired immediately to replace her. Malone and Embury were both trying to take a hand in directing the organizing and neither had much success. Their orders to organizers were often at cross purposes and confusion resulted. Organizers soon began to drift away, complaining about top-level interference with their work and a lack of clear direction. Party figures indicate memberships had climbed from the previous year's 8,000 to over 17,000, but even if those figures are accurate (membership figures are easy to manipulate and tend not to be a good indicator of party strength), they were still far behind the other parties' claims.

In the background, a federal-provincial fight over money was brewing. Provincial officials felt the federal controllers of the fund were not giving the provincial party all it deserved as quickly as possible. The provincial party had to overdraw at the bank to pay its summer bills and negotiations were going nowhere. On August 8, Embury made a public statement about the dispute, claiming Lang was holding the money up and exercising the control which provincial Liberals had feared when the fund was established. Federal Liberal officials quickly countered that Lang was not involved and any delay in dividing the money was purely administrative and not a matter for public debate. Shortly after, the dispute was settled and Embury got his money, but federal officials — and some provincial officials — were furious that it had become a matter of public controversy. The federal-provincial, Malone-Lang rift grew.

By August, Malone felt it was time to step out of the race briefly to consider the state of the party. He took his ten caucus colleagues and headed for Waskesiu, a northern Saskatchewan resort area, for three days of seclusion and debate over party principles, which could be shared and expanded to act as a base for the party's revival. It was not a time for debate of short-term tactics or party organization. Instead, it was set up as a time for reflection. "The broad purpose," said one participant in the closed session, "was to rediscover our purpose." For three days, the MLAs articulated concerns about big and growing government, the power of labor unions, the public apathy about politics. The debate was disjointed and without focus or conclusion, but Malone emerged to tell reporters he and other Liberals were concerned about the low esteem felt for politics and politicians by members of the public. It was not the sort of statement to attract wide attention but party officials were satisfied that they had at least been able to debate something beyond the latest crisis. They did the same thing several weeks later in a two-day meeting in Moose Jaw. However, even that attempt to escape the signs of decline failed. During the Waskesiu caucus, the isolated peacefulness of the setting was pierced by the news of two more desertions. MLAs Glen Penner (Saskatoon Eastview) and Bill Stodalka (Maple Creek) said they would not run again because they wanted to return to their jobs as school superintendents. Merchant and Cameron were still talking about running federally and thirteen-year veteran Cy MacDonald, the only remaining caucus member from the Thatcher government, was letting it be known he planned to quit when the next election was called.

The caucus was steadily shrinking and Malone seemed unable to stop it. September brought to a head the Merchant-Cameron defection plan. During the year, the two federally-oriented MLAs had joined with some federal Liberals in devising a "scenerio" to return momentum to the provincial Liberals. Basically, it called for Merchant and Cameron to run federally in a fall 1977 federal election and win. This would open the way for two by-elections and the momentum from the federal victories would lead to provincial by-election wins. The provincial party would be on the move again. The plan was based on a number of "ifs" but some in the party thought it would work. "We felt we needed that kind of dramatic shot in the arm to get back momentum," said Glen Penner later. But there were skeptics who felt it was just an easy way for Merchant and Cameron to abandon what they considered a sinking cause in search of easier victories. Federal Liberal fortunes seemed on the rise in the province at the time, and when both MLAs announced September 30 they were running federally to contribute to the fight for national unity, it rang in as opportunism to many. Former leader Steuart, the federal campaign chairman for the province, said he opposed the idea from the beginning and he thought Malone should have as well. Instead, Malone was briefed on the "scenerio" and did not raise a fight. "If I had been Ted, I would have taken the provincial party right out of the organization but he didn't object," said Steuart. "When they left, the life went out of the party. People were telling me if you can't keep your better members, why should we support you?"

It was another blow to the party image and if, as everyone expected, a federal election was called for the fall, the Liberals would drop to nine seats and third-party status in the Legislature. Out of fifteen Liberals elected little more than two years before, just eleven remained in the Legislature and Malone could count on just six of them to run for re-election.

As fall began, reports to party headquarters were making it clear the costly gamble of hiring full-time organizers for the countryside was not paying off. News was filtering back that the Conservatives were a strong presence almost everywhere while Liberals were hard to find. "The Conservatives did a good job," one Liberal organizer in Saskatoon said later. "While were we electing a leader, fighting those by-elections and then lying back, the Tories were out selling memberships. They even approached our defeated candidates." Organizers were also reporting back that the legacy of the leadership race was still a burden. Many of the executive members of riding associations across the province had been elected the year before as part of a slate of leadership convention delegates. Their main interest was the leadership, and when the convention was over, they were unwilling to carry on the necessary groundwork for the rest of the year. Organizations became dormant and some were not even planning annual meetings in 1977.

With the organization in shambles, the party turned to matters of policy in an attempt to begin the process of election-platform formulation started at the Waskesiu caucus in August. First, a "thinkers' conference" was held in Saskatoon October 11 to give party personnel and outside "experts" like former federal Auditor General Maxwell Henderson a chance to talk about the "challenges for tomorrow." The speeches and comments centred on the threat of big government and big labor. Malone left the meeting proclaiming it was the beginning of a philosophical renewal for the party which would become a "positive force" divorced from the negativism of the Thatcher and Steuart years. The one-day affair also won the party some badly-needed publicity.

Then, three weeks later, the seventy-second annual Liberal convention was held at the Saskatoon Centennial Auditorium. Malone used it as a showcase to outline some personal policies — a plan to turn provincially-owned resource crown corporations into private companies with shares for sale; a proposal to establish a commission to plan a streamlining of government if Liberals were elected; and implementation of zero-based budgeting and establishment of a program auditor to make sure that government programs served a purpose or were phased out. These policy ideas were well received and approved by delegates. They also passed some resolutions calling for improvement in the administration of justice and favoring creation of a system of Indian self-government on reserve lands.

However, although the convention was billed as a rebuilding session and efforts were made to drum up enthusiasm among the estimated 680 delegates, it was generally a quiet, reserved affair. The party decline and Tory surge dominated more hallway conversations than Liberal prospects in the next election. Party leaders acknowledged the talk with some statements of their own. Both Malone and Embury attacked Liberals who were openly talking about making a deal with the Tories as the best way to beat the NDP next time. "We have to stand up to the enemy within, the small group of Liberals who talk about making a deal with the Tories or not fighting hard in 1979 but waiting until 1983 or 1987," Malone said in one speech. "As long as I'm leader of this party, there will be no deal with the Tories."

Embury also attacked the defeatist thinkers. "There are those pessimists who maintain that we as a party are in decline and that we are wasting our time, effort and money in building up our organization at this time," he told delegates in his annual president's report. "I do not accept that premise and I do not think there is room in our party for this kind of pessimistic thinking." Delegates cheered the defiance, but their spirits had to be dampened a little by the financial news. In 1977, a year when almost everything had gone wrong and the party had lost substantial ground, it had spent close to $180,000 more than it collected. Although delegates were not told the total news, the truth was the party had been reduced to almost no cash assets. Its major asset was the party headquarters building purchased in the early seventies. The expensive and unsuccessful attempt to send organizers into the countryside had eaten into the party kitty, and Malone was not an effective fund-raiser. He looked more and more to the federal rebate scheme for funds. The once well-oiled and financed provincial machine had indeed fallen on hard times.

Less than two weeks later, November 16, the Legislature opened, and for the first time, Liberals had to share their Opposition standing with the PCs. Liberal MLAs were prepared to shine in the House, hoping finally to turn the spotlight back onto their party. It was not to be. The day the session opened, Tory Whip Eric Berntson delivered a letter to Speaker John Brockelbank charging collusion between the NDP and Liberals in planning seating in the Legislature because the Liberals had been placed at the Speaker's immediate left. That is the spot traditionally reserved for the official Opposition and since they were tied, Berntson argued the PCs should have had a chance to take that spot. The NDP immediately charged Berntson had accused the Speaker of being involved in the collusion and for the next two months the issue received extensive House debate. A little-used standing committee convened to consider if the privileges of the House had been breached, Tories refused to attend, and in the end, two PC MLAs were suspended for five days for not cooperating and for calling the committee a kangaroo court. In January, Berntson was also suspended for five days for not retracting a charge of political deal-making. It was, in the end, an old-boys' debate which meant little to voters (except to convince a few that the PCs did not respect the traditions and rules of the Legislature). But for the Liberals, the effect was negative. While they continued to perform well in the House, hammering away at government policies, dominating question period, and arguing for changes in agricultural and resource policies, better law enforcement, and improved treatment for native people, the PCs continued to grab the headlines, either for their antics or through attacks on them by the government.

Another chance came for the Liberals when on November 23, Bill 42, the key piece of 1973 legislation aimed at collecting higher oil royalties and exerting more government control over the oil industry, was declared unconstitutional by the Supreme Court of Canada. It was potentially a damaging blow for the NDP, which based its image on good resource management. Close to half a billion dollars had been collected in royalties under Bill 42 and the immediate threat of the court ruling was that it would have to be paid back. The government quickly announced it would be introducing retroactive tax legislation to make sure the money was retained by the government. Would the ruling make the public uneasy about the management ability of the NDP? Would voters find the prospect of retroactive legislation distasteful? It seemed to be a gold mine for the Opposition parties, although they also had to tread carefully. Both immediately said the government should not pay back the money because it would bankrupt the province. But there were many other areas in which to score debating points, and with the PCs playing their usual game of taking little part in the debate, the Liberals had a good opportunity to shine. During the close to 1½ months of debate on the legislation, they did usually dominate Opposition debate. However, it was not an impressive display of logic or consistency.

Malone at first argued the way to preserve the money was not to legislate but to go to the companies and negotiate. The idea was ridiculed by many who suggested the government would not be arguing from strength if it did that. As the debate wore on in the Legislature, Liberals took the stand that they would not support the bill unless the government could prove it was consititutional. The government refused, and in fact, the Liberal proposal would have kept the uncertainty going for months as the government sought an opinion from the Supreme Court of Canada. What the industry felt was needed quickly was a decision and some certainty about the new rules of the oil business. Liberals proposed a few other delaying amendments, and when second reading approval in principle came December 22, the Liberals opposed it while the NDP and PCs combined to approve it. The Legislature reconvened early in the new year to finish work on the bill, and by then, the PCs were doing more talking. On January 12, the bill received final approval with only the Liberals opposing it. PC leader Collver and government spokesmen made strong speeches about the need for provincial taxing powers over resources. Malone ended his contribution with a strange speech. He said Liberals did not want the government to give the money back to the oil companies, but his alternative was unclear. "We believe the oil industry should be paying every last penny in taxes the government can gouge out of them," he said. "But at the same time, there must be some room for the industry to gain a fair return on its investment in this province."

It was not a strong stand and it had not been a strong session for Liberals. The chance to score impressive points on the resource issue appeared to elude the Liberals and they failed again to dominate the public stage. At the same time, the PCs had been able to reinforce in the public mind the idea that the Liberals and NDP were cooperating to stop the surge of the Tories.

Inside the Liberal party, officials were preoccupied with trying to find out what was going wrong. Malone had been leader for a year and the party slide had turned into an avalanche. He seemed unable to motivate the party, despite travel and some hard work. "Ted was certainly trying in '77," said President Embury. "He was trying to motivate people but they just wouldn't work." Dick Mundy, hired from Ontario in November to be executive director, said he found the party dispirited when he arrived. "When I came out, all I kept hearing was the Tory groundswell," he said. "You had to believe it was true." MLA Glen Penner said caucus members were depressed after a year of setbacks and worry about their re-election chances. "There was so much talk about everyone going Tory that it hurt the morale of those of us who had been elected," he said later.

What had happened to the optimism of the previous December when a new leader was elected and a new leaf turned? A number of things had happened and many of them were out of the control of Malone or other party leaders. The bitterness and divisions of the leadership race were deep and lasting, the momentum of the PCs was under full steam and difficult to stop, and a combination of personal aspirations and timing had conspired to deliver a series of setbacks to the party which damaged its image and added gravity to the inward collapse of the party. In many ways, Malone had been a victim rather than a villain.

However, some of the blame also had to fall on the man who campaigned so hard to win the mantle of leadership. During his first year in office, flaws in his experience, political savvy, techniques, and personality made him less than an effective leader for a party in need of a lift.

Party insiders and critics suggest the first mistake he made was in not having a clear idea of where he wanted to go once the leadership race was won. "There seemed to be no plan to stop reacting and start planning for the future," said Merchant. Former leader Steuart says while Malone talked to him about some aspects of the job, he never asked for advice on how to actually run a party. "Ted never really sat down with me and said 'How does the organization work?' " Steuart said. "I don't think he had a grasp on the job, how large it was, how complex it was, how many people it took."

Insiders also paint a picture of him as a man largely unwilling to take advice, expecting deference as leader. While he ran caucus as a consensus operation, rather than a dictatorship, he left many convinced he expected them to implement orders, not take part in the decision-making. He failed to include many Liberals who had opposed him in the leadership race and isolated himself from many who thought they could contribute to formulation of a direction for the party. "When people would complain about these things, he would just get defensive about it," said Merchant. "Ted is not a listener. Ted is not a consulter."

Perhaps his most serious flaw as leader was his lack of organizational understanding. Malone liked to tell people about his success directing the 1971 and 1967 campaigns for Don McPherson in Regina Lakeview. However, that was a traditional Liberal urban seat and many of the lessons of those campaigns could not be applied provincially. Malone began his leadership years woefully unfamiliar with both the province and the party structure outside Regina. Yet he insisted on taking a personal interest in most organization matters, often down to the smallest detail. It caused havoc at the organizer level and led to the departure of more than one worker. "Ted isn't an organizer but he doesn't know that," organizer Paul Taylor said later. "He is great in many areas, but he doesn't know his limitations." At one point in 1977, Malone was even having the organizers in the field call him each morning, and on more than one occasion, he reversed orders previously given to them by other party officials. "They were just going around in circles and just drifted away," said President Embury. "My only criticism of Ted is that he won't take advice. His basic flaw is that he doesn't trust other people."

He also did not understand how to treat them at times. Party workers complain he did not understand the fine points of massaging egos and inspiring through encouragement. "He always seemed to assume he deserved what we did for him," a key worker said. Similar stories of Malone's failure to take into account the human need for appreciation or encouragement came from executive members. Many party workers attributed it to an inherent shyness. Others thought it resulted from his upper-class background and a basic lack of empathy with other classes. Whatever the explanation, it led to mixed reviews for the leader from some of those he had to call on to help him maintain the party. "Some days, he's nice and good and he's up there with a halo," said organizer Taylor, who spent two years with the party. "Other days, I can't stand working for him. I hate the dirt he walks on."

Malone recognized some of the weaknesses in himself. He told an interviewer he had not deliberately tried to exclude Merchant supporters from a role in the party, but that had apparently happened anyway. "I must subconsciously exclude people or others wouldn't keep saying that," he said. He also conceded he did not take advice well, although he had a justification: "The advice I often get is 'Ross would have done this or Dave would have done that.' My response is 'yes, but look where it got them.'" Finally, he readily conceded he was not an organizer. "I'm basically a policy guy," he said.

Yet despite this awareness, he continued to commit the errors. Although he lacked instinctive organizational talents, he continued to try to play a direct and influential role in that side of the party. While the party needed a strong image and high profile, he seemed unable to provide either. He projected an image of honesty and sincerity, but those were not commodities in great demand at the time. The political events of the province and the aspirations of the population articulated by the politicians seemed to be passing Malone and the Liberals by.

As 1978 settled over Saskatchewan, Liberal leaders decided to try a different tactic. There was a general assumption it was federal election year and federal Liberal chances in the province seemed to be on the rise. For the first time in years, provincial Liberals decided to try to ride on federal coattails. They would work hard for the feds and if they scored gains, the momentum would transfer to the provincial party. "The thinking was 'we're down. What can we do? Let's see what the feds can do,' " Malone said. In the meantime, he planned to travel the province trying to patch together riding organizations, find candidates, and begin the building process for the 1979 provincial vote. The long-range strategy was that a platform of policies would be decided at a fall convention and Malone would spend the next winter in a high-profile move around the province, trying to get exposure and recognition.

This scenerio led to a serious mistake. The provincial party, with the urging of some federal officials, decided to delay nominating candidates until after a federal election. It was a drastic reversal for Malone who just months earlier had been advocating early nomination of candidates. "In the long run, I think the earlier the nomination the better, particularly in the rural areas because in the wintertime, the candidate is normally going around to bonspiels, auctions, dances and so on," he told an interviewer. "He's going to be doing that anyway so he can be campaigning at the same time. As soon as there is a candidate declared in a constituency, I will be pushing that constituency to hold a nominating convention."

What had happened? Malone says it was federal intervention. He says in October 1977, federal campaign chairman Senator Steuart contacted him to ask that provincial candidates not be nominated in case they should cause confusion in the mind of the voter with a federal campaign expected. Later, Malone said, federal Transport Minister Lang called and made the same request, and finally a representative of the prime minister's office called. Malone had decided the best chance was to feed off federal successes anyway so he agreed. Federal officials involved do not all agree with Malone's version of the events. Senator Steuart says he did not specifically ask that candidates not be nominated, except in areas where there would be a difficult but winnable federal fight. He said that left many areas where candidates could have been nominated. He did, however, ask Malone not to be too aggressive in his fund-raising. "But if he got the message from me to lay off getting candidates, he was misinterpreting me," said Steuart. Lang was more supportive of the Malone version. "We did discuss it and agreed it made sense to hold off for a while until the federal thing was over," Lang said later. It may have made sense for the federal Liberals but for the provincial Liberals, it was a mistake. Both NDP and PC officials were stressing candidate nominations and the public perception was that the Liberals were not even in the race. By the end of the summer, PCs and NDP claimed more than a score of candidates nominated each. The Liberals had two. It was bad politics and, in the end, bad strategy. The Liberals were not following the basic political tactic of being ready for a fight at all times.

During the spring and summer, Malone was not leaving the quest for candidates completely untended. He travelled quietly around the province, trying to convince people to be ready to let their names stand when the time came. The response was not always encouraging. In many areas, he found riding organizations which could not produce a candidate and prospective candidates who were not willing to get involved so early or who wanted to wait for the federal election campaign first. In Saskatoon Buena Vista, for instance, Malone tried to convince lawyer Jim Serne to run. The riding executive and most workers were gearing up for the federal fight to re-elect Lang and Serne politely told Malone to come back later when the federal election was over. He had the same reception in other ridings.

Politically, the spring and summer of 1978 were quiet in the province as most eyes were turned on Ottawa and the expected federal campaign. A Legislature session began March 6 and, except for a record $1.6 billion budget and some amendments to provincial election spending law, it was quiet. Liberal MLAs criticized government spending plans while arguing for a tax break for farmers on fuel used in production of food or in other agricultural jobs. The Conservative MLAs were speaking more and playing a more active role in Legislature debates. They ended up being accused by both Liberal and NDP speakers of trying unnecessarily to prolong the session through frivolous debate in hopes a federal election would be called, Merchant and Cameron would have to quit to campaign, and the PCs would become the official Opposition.

It was a session characterized by some personal vindictiveness between parties and it ended in late May with Malone lamenting the "ugliness and bitterness" of the previous two months. Election Act amendments were approved to raise party election spending limits to $250,000 and constituency limits to the greater of one dollar a voter or $15,000. The law also provided for a rebate of up to $75,000 provincially for a party if it received 15 percent of the vote in an election and comparable rebates on individual constituency levels.

During the winter, the PCs had started to receive some damaging media coverage. First, several Liberals and NDP MLAs said in January they had been offered financial or political inducements by Collver if they would join his party. Collver said attempts to convince politicians to switch allegiance were politics as usual, but the episode appeared to indicate an underhanded side to Collver's tactics. A bitter legal fight between Collver and his former Saskatoon business partners over division of property was settled out of court during the winter, but allegations that Collver had misused some of the partnership money remained on the public record, unsubstantiated but damaging. Then in May, shortly after the first law suit was quietly settled, came the worst news — the government-owned Saskatchewan Government Insurance Office was suing Collver for $1.1 million, alleging he was responsible for the debts of a construction company he had sold to four Calgary men several years before. The company had defaulted on several construction projects which SGIO had to finish financing and the insurance company wanted some repayment. Collver immediately said the SGIO suit was a political move by a government agency to discredit him and he argued all his liability for the company had ended when he sold it. It seemed like a gold mine for Liberals in their fight for credibility. Publicly, they called for a Legislature investigation into Collver's charge that the suit was politically motivated. Privately, they were gleefully speculating about how the story would damage Collver's political stock and how they could use it without appearing to be too brutal or opportunistic.

This apparent piece of good fortune did not change the basic Liberal condition of unreadiness, however. Despite some low-key optimism about the Tory momentum having been either reversed or at least stopped, an organizational shambles stared Liberals in the face. "We have let the organization go and that is what wins elections," MLA Sonny Anderson said in late May. At one point, he had decided not to run again but the poor state of the party convinced him he should fight one more election to try to increase party chances.

While Liberals fretted about their sorry state of readiness, Saskatchewan's other two parties were in better shape. Both NDP and PCs had worked themselves into fighting trim for an expected federal election and the impact had filtered down to provincial organizations. Within the NDP, there were some concerns about the surging PCs and the collapsing Liberals, but party leaders were also receiving some encouraging news both from private poll results and from reports being sent in from the countryside — the party remained the most popular in the field, Blakeney was still widely respected (perhaps more so now in comparision to the Opposition), government resource policies were no longer controversial and had been accepted in many parts of the electorate, and the recent commitment to uranium development and greater development generally was creating a sense of optimism or complacency which would favor the party in any provincial vote. Organizations across the province were strong and candidates had either been chosen or were ready to stand in most ridings. Several veteran government members, including Revenue Minister Wes Robbins, were threatening not to run again, but it was not considered a major problem.

Conservatives were also confident. Their organizations were in fighting trim, money was flowing in, candidates had been lined up in most ridings, and expectations were that in a federal vote, most of the seats would be won by the PCs. Although federal and provincial campaigners said they were separate efforts, a strong federal showing would help provincial Tories. In the Legislature and in the country, the party was trying to develop a moralistic, law-and-order platform to discredit the government. MLA Gary Lane had talked about the need for prison reform to make the punishment side of the ledger more important. He complained that prisoners were being coddled and were becoming an "athletic elite" because of prison recreation programs, while prison guards and police were being demoralized. PCs also urged a national return to capital punishment and told voters the NDP was soft on the issue. However, there was one worrying development for the Tories. NDP efforts to discredit Collver appeared to be having an effect. The New Democrats were referring to allegations made against the

Conservative leader during court hearings, belittling his efforts in the Legislature, and urging voters to compare Blakeney and Collver before casting their votes.

Collver had privately told party leaders he would resign if they felt these allegations were hurting party chances but there was little stomach in the party for unseating the man who had made them a threat in less than five years. Collver helped quiet any doubts by making no move to step aside while decrying the NDP "smear campaign." He also successfully convinced many Conservatives that the party was on the verge of winning, despite the best NDP efforts to thwart the inevitable. Conservatives went into the summer optimistic.

As spring turned to summer and a federal election had still not been called, there were rumors that a provincial election might come instead. Several senior NDP officials told Malone and other senior Liberals in June that they might be facing a fall provincial vote if there was no federal election. The idea caused a minor panic among senior Liberals but few seriously believed there would be no federal vote. A campaign committee was set up to begin planning strategy but during the next two months, it met only a few times. In late summer, Penner and MacDonald said publicly what party insiders had known for a year — they would not be running again.

September brought a sudden change to the political landscape. In Ottawa, Prime Minister Trudeau announced a series of economic measures to cut government spending and to reduce bureaucracy. He downplayed the possibility of a federal election that fall. Suddenly, a provincial election became not only possible but probable. The Liberals were in a panic. They had just two candidates nominated, no real election plan, just the vague beginnings of a policy platform, and at best a spotty organization which could not be considered dependable. "We weren't ready," said one MLA. "The election was just one more disaster."

In the early days of September, a policy committee was established to write a platform, the election committee began meeting at a feverish pace, and planning started on both a strategy and a leader's election tour.

The party was beginning a fight for its life and everyone knew it.

Chapter Thirteen

THE CAMPAIGN DISASTER, 1978

The decision to call an October 8 election was made by the provincial cabinet in early September, as soon as it became obvious a federal vote would not be called. The move was ratified by the NDP provincial council at a Regina meeting September 16 and announced to the province by Premier Blakeney September 19.

On the surface, it looked like a risky decison for the government to make. An antigovernment mood had been reflected in provincial elections and public opinion polls across the country for months. The Conservative strength seemed to be much in evidence and in some ways, the NDP appeared to be running scared. But in the privacy of their meeting, NDP leaders had some compelling reasons for calling an early election. They feared the party would not be able to afford both a federal and provincial election in 1979, and despite the public uncertainty, they felt they could win a fall vote. Private polls for the party showed the NDP with 45 percent of the decided voters while the Conservatives trailed with 35 percent and the Liberals held 20 percent. There was also a distrust of the PC leader Collver, and party strategists felt they could swing many of the uncommitted to their side with a skillful attack on both Collver and the Conservative record in other provinces. The NDP felt it could win the election on the issues of leadership, health care, and resource management, and with a financial bonanza expected within a few years as the provincial uranium industry developed, it looked as if the winner of the next election could hold power for years with money to fund the programs which keep the voters happy.

One aspect of the poll results and the public mood troubled some NDP planners. How far would the Liberal collapse go and where would the Liberal votes find a home if the party did collapse? A stampede to the Conservatives as the "free enterprise" alternative to the NDP would be bad news. They were not encouraged when Deputy Premier Roy Romanow and Provincial Secretary Elwood Cowley, two of the NDP's leading political tacticians, met with veteran Liberal Cy MacDonald in early September to warn him that a mid-October election might be coming. MacDonald told them it might be a mistake. The Liberals were weaker than the NDP poll showed and a Liberal rout could hurt the NDP. "Cy was trying to save the party, give it a bit more time," a member of the Liberal election committee said later. The message wasn't entirely lost on the NDP. "The most significant thing about this election was that we would destroy the Liberal Party," NDP campaign manager Bill Knight said after the election. "We knew that when it was called."

Some Liberals had similar fears. As the election writ was being issued, pollsters working for Tony Merchant were sampling the opinions of more than 1,800 Saskatchewan voters. Their analysis of the mid-September voter mood came a few weeks later and it showed the Liberals with about 15 percent of the popular vote, running third in most ridings and second in a handful. Not one Liberal was shown as leading, including party leader Malone. These results might have been of some help had they been generally known within party planning circles. Instead, Merchant considered the information his own unless someone asked about it, and by the end of the campaign, just a few senior Liberals had figured out the code and heard the bad news.

Even without precise poll results, however, senior Liberals knew the desperate situation they were in. Election planning in the days prior to the election call and immediately after was aimed at developing a policy platform and finding sixty-one candidates.

The search for candidates was the greatest immediate challenge. By September 18, the day before the election call, the NDP had nominated forty candidates and said it expected the rest to be nominated by September 25. The PCs had nominated thirty-four, excluding their eleven sitting MLAs. The Liberals had nominated three. Public and media speculation was widespread that the party would not be able to field a full slate of candidates. To have any credibility with the voters, the party had to begin finding candidates and the job went primarily to Embury, with help from Malone and Executive Director Mundy. The deadline for filing nomination papers was October 2 and for the two weeks preceding that date, prospective candidates were cajoled, pressured, promised, and pursued. "It was critical to have sixty-one candidates," said Embury. "We would have had no credibility without it."

In reality, the situation was not as bad as it appeared on the surface. Malone and Embury had convinced about forty people to stand before the election call and it was simply a matter of having a convention to get them nominated. The remaining twenty were more difficult and the last three or four were almost impossible. Embury travelled, telephoned, and called in as many obligations as the party could find to convince people to run. Malone would often spend several hours on the telephone as well when he finished his day of campaigning.

In the end, the effort was successful. When Bill Taylor agreed to run in

Redberry in late September, the Liberals had their full slate. Malone capped the drive with his own Regina Lakeview nomination September 30 and he chided all those who had doubted it could be done. The Liberals hoped the full slate would give them instant credibility, and of course it did not. However, it was a major accomplishment and to have failed would have been a disaster.

The campaign for candidates included one incredible episode, a sequence of events Embury was later to joke was "the most expensive recruiting attempt in the history of Saskatchewan." It involved the attempt by Liberals in the Regina South constituency, held in the former Legislature by Liberal Stuart Cameron, to attract the well-known lawyer Morris Shumiatcher as a candidate. They felt the appearance of a name candidate would save the seat for the party, even though they were starting off behind. Shumiatcher had been interested in the nomination and told them he would run in a summer 1979 election, according to party officials. When the snap fall election was called, he was touring Australia and Japan. Riding officials finally tracked him down in Japan and telexed him. Shumiatcher telexed back that he would not run, but the riding executive was not to be dissuaded. After several more telexes failed to win his commitment, they collected enough money and sent a representative of the riding executive to Japan with the nomination papers for Shumiatcher to sign. He still refused and an embarrassed Liberal had to return to Regina empty-handed and in need of a candidate.

Regina South was not the only riding where the early election call deterred potential candidates who had committed themselves to running in a June 1979 race. Despite that, the Liberals managed to assemble a credible team by nomination day, including some rural mayors and local personalities. The party even convinced Cy MacDonald to run one more time in Indian Head-Wolseley. The veteran of fourteen years in the Legislature had wanted out but party loyalty and the lack of an attractive alternative Liberal candidate brought him back for one more election.

The process of developing a policy was not as high-pressure but it was just as rushed. In the first two weeks of September, the election and policy committees wrote a platform that normally would have taken months to evolve. The end result was the most unusual policy to be offered by a Saskatchewan political party in years. It proposed a series of referenda giving the voters a chance to crack down on unions and the right to strike, reduce the size of governments, and establish a series of run-off elections in any constituency in which the winning candidate received less than 50 percent of the votes. Its roots were part Ross Thatcher and part European democracy, a combination of traditional Liberal party concerns and a political attempt to find an unusual alternative which would catch the voters' attention and focus the spotlight on the Liberals. The platform planners were as much concerned with catching attention and pandering to what they perceived as the public's right-wing mood as they were with reflecting liberalism. In the end, it was a gamble which did not work. Its failure left Liberals with an even more confused idea about what the party represented.

The roots of the policy lay in a series of meetings held by Liberal officials and MLAs during 1977 and 1978, beginning with the Waskesiu caucus in August 1977, the "thinkers conference" and annual convention in Saskatoon during the fall, and a June 1978 caucus meeting in Swift Current. Out of these meetings and a late summer voter issues poll, three general themes began to emerge. Participants sensed that growing government and its eroding effect on personal freedom, workplace disruptions caused by unions, and disrespect for politicians were the three main issues on the public mind. They were essentially conservative reactions to the growth of government, social programs, and worker power during the past decade, and while Liberals had been anxious to jump on those earlier bandwagons when they were in favor, they were now equally ready to abandon them in disfavor and to play to public suspicions. The California voter tax revolt in summer 1978 also had an impact on Liberal planners as they surveyed the desolation of their party and considered how to win voter support.

But how could the Liberal party tap those forces? Stuart Cameron says the idea came to him on the drive back to Regina after the June Swift Current caucus. "I realized our thinking was still too loose. It lacked reality," he said. Cameron began to consider the possibility of a referenda policy which would outline the problems and then ask the voters to give a Liberal government the power to make dramatic changes. He mentioned it to a few friends, including Merchant, but the idea lay dormant for several months. In early September, Malone called Cameron to ask if he would serve on a policy committee and Cameron agreed. He then raised the referenda idea in a meeting with Malone and policy director Harold MacKay in Malone's office. "I told them I thought the referendum idea was the instrument we needed," Cameron said later. The idea was taken to the election committee and the politicians took over, planning the specifics and deciding how to present it to the public with the most impact.

By mid-September, the basic plan had been settled. There would be three proposals for referenda around which the campaign would be centred. They would be announced one at a time at news conferences around the province during the first three weeks of the campaign. First would be a proposal on government reorganization — a newly-elected Liberal government would freeze government spending and hiring, freeze taxes and government-controlled utility rates, introduce zero-based budgetting, and try to streamline government. On March 5, 1979, voters would have a chance to approve a proposal that government spending be reduced by 15 percent, with specific areas of cutting to be decided by the voters. The second would be a proposal on labor relations — the government would immediately outlaw strikes in essential services, pass laws to allow a ninety-day cooling-off period before any strike, and change the make-up of the Labor Relations Board. Then on June 18, 1979, a referendum would be held on whether to abolish the right to strike completely and replace it with compulsory arbitration. The third referendum would deal with reform of the electoral system. On October 15, 1979, voters would be asked to approve a system of run-off elections in which any candidate who did not receive 50 percent of the vote would have to face his nearest rival in a run-off shortly after the initial election.

The referenda policy was to prove the most controversial — and for many, bewildering — aspect of the Liberal campaign. The platform was to include proposals on other topics, such as Malone's idea to turn government resource companies into private firms with shares sold to the public. But the central theme was to be the three referenda and the "Year of Decision" in which the votes would be held.

Unlike the preparation for the 1975 election, the 1978 policy was not the outgrowth of intensive party membership study or outcry on the issues. The topics were chosen by a handful of planners. The government reform and labor policies had some obvious roots in the party past and in the public mood many politicians perceived. They came primarily from Merchant and Cameron. The run-off scheme was more obscure, and for many people, baffling. The idea came from President Embury who thought it a way to restore faith in government by making sure the winners had majority support, even if some of those supporters voted for the winner as the lesser of two evils on the second ballot.

Even as the platform was being planned, Liberal officials recognized it had two major drawbacks. Since the ideas were new, many voters might dismiss them as simple political expediency, doubting Liberal sincerity. And because they were so unusual, voters might be confused or turned off the Liberals because they could not understand the platform.

The party had reason to be concerned on both counts. In fact, the referenda policy was in large part based on expediency. Members of the committee involved in writing the policy readily admit their eye was as much on the voter mood as it was on party principles. "We didn't just do it to catch attention," said Malone. "But when you're into a campaign, you try to get a policy people will be talking about." Embury said there was fear the Liberals would get lost on the sidelines if the election developed into a test of will between the NDP and PCs. They had to have something to make them different, to make the media and the voters and, they hoped, other parties pay attention to them. "We were trying to sound different from the Tories and the idea of referendums sounded very appealing," he said. "It was also considered a credible way to deal with the desire to cut back government and to deal with labor problems." Merchant would later call it "media event policy."

To counter skepticism about the conversion to referenda, planners evolved the argument that it was really just an extension of traditional liberal concern for the rights and voice of the individual. One problem with the argument was that Malone was demonstrably a recent convert. In a Legislature speech on May 2, 1977, in reaction to a Conservative proposal for a public vote on the seat-belt issue, Malone said: "I think they [referenda] are really the politician's cop-out. Those who haven't got the guts to make up their own minds as to the goodness or badness of a particular law always go out and take the easy way out and say 'well let's have a referendum about it.' I don't think . . . that we are elected to sit in this House to always run to the public for a referendum as soon as a politically contentious issue arises." During the campaign, Malone tried to argue he had had a change of opinion but those words came back to haunt him many times.

In the end, the platform had to be seen as a desperate attempt to be different, eye-catching, and in line with the assumed public move to the right. It combined the conservatism of Ross Thatcher with the republicanism of direct referenda balloting. It had little link with the roots of the party or the political culture of the province. It was an imaginative, slick, and totally inadequate attempt at policy making.

It was also hard to explain in the twenty-eight days the campaign allowed. The concept was a new one for Saskatchewan voters and it would have taken months of explaining and persuading even to get a full hearing. Party leaders did not help matters by not giving the full party executive or the candidates advance warning. They heard the platform announced piecemeal on the radio with the rest of the voters, and the result was confusion. Candidates who were expected to explain and defend the ideas immediately often did not understand them or agree with them. In some ridings, candidates refused to include discussion of them in their campaigning.

The party explanation for the lack of forewarning and candidate education was a lack of time and the need for secrecy to have the best effect on voters and the media. It also showed arrogance and bad planning which reduced what little chance the policy had to have an impact on voters.

Although finding candidates and writing a policy were early election priorities, the Liberals also had a campaign to run from Day One. Considering the confusion and panic which characterized the behind-the-scenes planning, the public campaign was in many ways more successful than anyone thought possible at the beginning. After an uncertain start, Malone turned into an effective campaigner. The strategy was flexible enough to allow him to react to immediate events, and on the surface, it often looked as if the Liberals were successfully making an impression, forcing voters to consider again the traditional alternative to the NDP.

From the beginning, Liberal officials had no delusions about winning. "We began just wanting to hold what we had," said an organizer. "There was almost no hope of picking any up." It was considered a fight to maintain a solid, dependable base for the rebuilding job which would be necessary after the election. They decided at the start not to repeat the 1975 mistake of trying to spread the leader too thin. Malone would concentrate his efforts in the potentially winnable areas of the southern and western sections of the province. Any venture into the cities, central, or northern areas would be brief and mainly aimed at convincing the media that the party was not giving up on any areas. To try to counter voter ignorance of Liberal policies and the lack of local organizations to spread the word, Malone's tour was heavily dependent on aircraft which allowed him to visit widely separate locations the same day.

However, strategists planning his travels had one unwelcome problem to consider. Malone was facing a strong challenge in Regina Lakeview and would have to spend more time than normal for a leader in his seat, trying to ensure a personal victory. It made travel planning difficult and required that the leader be back in Regina almost every night for a bit of late-night or early-morning personal campaigning.

Within twenty-four hours of Blakeney's September 19 election call, the campaigning was on and the leaders were laying down their general principles and campaign strategies. Blakeney said the issue was resource development and the expected flood of dollars from potash, oil, and uranium development in the immediate future. "The old-line parties believe Saskatchewan should be satisfied with the jobs and economic activity which comes from resource development and not seek high royalties," he told reporters. "The NDP believes the resources belong to the people of Saskatchewan, this generation and future generations and royalties should be as high as is consistent with vigorous and sustained development." It quickly became plain the NDP considered the PCs the only real opposition, and within days, ads appeared suggesting the Conservatives would disrupt the medicare plan, reintroduce deterrent fees on health care, and give away the province to the corporate sector. Coupled with these fear-politics tactics (several of which even the NDP later conceded were less than honest) were the usual give-away promises — renters' rebates, farm fuel rebates, a tax break for senior citizens and homeowners, and an extension of some medicare programs. Voters were being told the NDP would offer responsible resource management, an extension of the welfare state, and preservation of gains which had been made in the past. They also made subtle but effective efforts to convince voters that because of his various court dealings and the outstanding suit by SGIO, PC leader Collver was slightly shady.

The PC campaign was much more low-key than many had expected. They promised a purge of "politically-appointed" civil servants to cut the fat and increase morale among career civil servants; a reduction in taxes and the size of government; a re-examination of welfare policies; decentralization of power with more authority being passed to local governments; and an increase in senior citizen incomes to tie them to the provincial minimum wage. Conservatives tried to counter the attacks against Collver by ignoring them, but when the issue of the private affairs kept cropping up, the leader announced that a blind trust for his assets had been established, to be administered by former Supreme Court Justice Emmett Hall of Saskatoon. Collver also pledged that if elected premier, he would not interfere in the SGIO court case against him.

The PC tactic was essentially to appeal for less government and a new approach to resource management, accompanied by more power and money for local governments and provision of greater welfare state benefits to senior citizens. The PC pledge to set up private companies to take over from Crown resource companies and then to give company shares to Saskatchewan residents was controversial, but as the campaign progressed, Conservatives found to their dismay that Collver himself was the major issue. Voters appeared to be judging the party primarily through their view of the honesty and competence of its leader. The NDP was doing all it could to ensure their judgment was negative.

This battle between the NDP and PCs was both good and bad news for the Liberals. If the NDP could stop the Tory surge and discredit Collver, the Liberals could pick up some of the anti-NDP vote which had leaned Conservative. However, there were obvious dangers that the Liberals would seem irrelevant in such a two-way battle. Malone began the campaign by outlining the referenda policy and announcing the first would deal with big government and the Liberal pledge to "fundamentally" alter attitudes to government by "cutting it off at the knees." He tantalized reporters by promising more details on the other two referenda in later weeks. Malone hoped to draw the other parties into a debate on his ideas and challenged both Blakeney and Collver to issue position statements on big government, labor relations, and resource policies. Instead, there was little reaction and Malone spent much of the campaign doggedly explaining his positions while the main event of the election debate appeared to be happening elsewhere.

A pleasant surprise for the party was the way Malone grew as a campaigner. He appeared uncertain at first, afraid to confront voters face to face, and ineffective at mainstreeting. His early campaign technique was to stride into selected business establishments, march into the back office to huddle with the owner or manager, and then leave with little effort to make contact with the employees or customers who would be collectively more important on voting day. Malone seemed uncomfortable in the role of flesh-presser and he appeared to be seeking out the familiarity of the back rooms and managerial atmosphere. "Malone frequently told people campaigning was his favorite aspect of politics," a reporter covering the campaign said later. "The rest of his political career must be pure hell." Yet as the campaign wore on, Malone become better, more aggressive in his personal contacts, more confident and reassuring in his public speeches.

Throughout the campaign, the Liberals were forced to cope with suggestions they were irrelevent to the election. Collver consistently refused to comment on Liberal proposals, arguing the election was a straight fight between PCs and the NDP. The media also played that theme occasionally and Malone was often forced to predict, almost plead, that soon the other parties would be "aiming their guns at us." It didn't quite happen that way, although his policy proposals did attract occasional fire. When he announced the details of his labor policy during the second week, including right-to-work legislation, an end to union shops in which all new workers must join the union, and possible restrictions on international unions in the province, Saskatchewan Federation of Labor Executive Secretary Larry Brown charged that it was just a revival of Thatcher-era policies, being proposed for political gain. "He is desperate to get himself a few votes and he is looking for the most public issue that he can fasten onto to get a few votes." Malone countered that union members would not be as negative as their leaders, but in fact the Liberals had written off the union vote and decided to try to cash in on what they saw as public antipathy towards unions.

In the middle of the campaign, the Supreme Court of Canada issued a ruling which declared unconstitutional a key piece of provincial resource legislation — the potash prorationing law which gave the province the right to regulate production levels and the minimum price for potash produced in Saskatchewan. The law had been passed in 1969 under Ross Thatcher and defended in court by the NDP. News of the court decision at first seemed good for the opposition parties, and both Liberals and PCs said it showed the NDP were poor resource managers. It gave Malone another chance to say the government should try to settle its differences with the resource companies through negotiation and not legislation. Blakeney took a tough stand, attacking federal policies, aiming subtle barbs at the Supreme Court, and pledging to fight for provincial resource rights against the centralists in Ottawa. As had happened so often in the past, the anti-Ottawa tactic worked and the resource issue was essentially neutralized as a weapon to use against the government.

Two and a half weeks into the campaign, Malone unveiled his last referendum idea — the run-offs to ensure majority support for every winning candidate. Using the argument that most CCF-NDP governments had been elected with less than 50 percent of the popular vote, he said the province had been subjected to "socialism by default." He promoted his scheme as a way to ensure the NDP would be relegated to second-party, and perhaps third-party, status. "The majority feel they are impotent to stop the growth of socialism in Saskatchewan," he told reporters. "We seek this mandate because of our belief that the existing electoral process is failing." But to Liberal dismay, the idea failed to excite. Except for one Blakeney comment that it was unappealing and a *Saskatoon Star-Phoenix* story that one university constitutional law professor said the idea could be unconstitutional, no one paid it much attention. The final policy ace in the hole had fallen flat. Either it was not understood or people agreed with Blakeney that the Liberals were looking for a way to salvage a few votes when they could not win elections under the traditional parliamentary system.

While Malone was unveiling the planks of the official Liberal platform, the election committee was meeting frequently in Regina, looking for ways to turn the election around and get the party into the fight. By early October, they were conceding an NDP victory and trying to decide how best to level their guns at the PCs. One of the few committee members who suggested the election might still be winnable was Stuart Cameron. In an October 5 memo to Malone and the committee, he suggested a new approach to attacks on Collver — try to convince the people he was not committed to private enterprise. "A full 30 percent or 40 percent of the electorate remains undecided at this stage of the campaign," he wrote. "The bulk of the people want to change this government. They are undecided as between the Liberals and Conservatives." He suggested the party begin to accuse the PC leader of being "soft on free enterprise." Within a week, that message was appearing in Malone speeches and in the Liberal ad campaign, which was masterminded by Merchant.

The committee decided in the late stages to try one last tactic to lure voters to the Liberals. If voters could be convinced a bandwagon Liberal effect was developing, the reasoning went, a few more of them would decide to jump on. By October 14, newspaper ads were calling Malone the man who "turned things around." The message was that despite attempts by the "pundits and editorial writers" to count the Liberals out in the early days of the campaign, they were back in the race. "Now, everybody is talking about us." That night in Carlyle, a small community in southeastern Saskatchewan, Malone tried to drive the point home. "A lot has happened in these last three and a half weeks," he told the small crowd out to hear him.

The last few days of the campaign were strangely low-key for the Liberals. Malone made a few trips to small communities in the Regina area, predicting a close election and a good Liberal vote. He often apologized for not having been in the ridings often enough to help out the local candidate but attributed it to the short campaign. It was a message of hope, almost defiance, which he was giving in those final days. Privately, most of the senior Liberals had decided the party could win between five and ten seats election night and they were pleased. "We've come a hell of a long way since the beginning," Embury said two days before the election. "I know we came a lot farther than anyone expected us to. What we have demonstrated is that no matter what people say, when it comes to the crunch, there are a lot of Liberals out there." Embury and others felt the campaign had successfully kept a solid base of support intact and that would provide a good beginning for post-election work.

The media, though, were not convinced. Throughout the campaign, senior Liberals had complained bitterly about stories and newspaper columns which downplayed Liberal chances. Riding profiles often showed the Liberals in trouble or out of the race. Malone was often painted as someone the voters did not recognize. On October 16, the *Regina Leader-Post* published its pre-election editorial and it was more bad news for the Liberals. "Despite a hastily-organized comeback try, the Liberals under Ted Malone don't seem to have quite achieved a real position of serious, contention in the skirmishing," said the editorial. "It's still largely a battle of words and ideas and promises between the resurgent, well organized Conservatives under Dick Collver and Allan Blakeney's defense-counterattack strategy." Informal radio polls being published in the last week also showed the Liberals running third.

On October 17, Malone made his last campaign trip — a visit to Moose Jaw for a luncheon speech. On the way back to Regina by car, he told reporters he expected a minority government to be elected and he would be willing to talk to the Conservatives about cooperating in the Legislature if such a move was needed to keep the NDP out of power. His musings were published election day.

Election day, October 18, was sunny throughout most of Saskatchewan and, as usual, close to 80 percent of the eligible voters made their trek to the polling booths. Malone spent the day in his own riding, visiting a few polls, voting for the television cameras at 10:00 A.M., and playing some tennis. Other leading Liberals wondered if they would have a party left the next day. Many said later their mood fluctuated wildly during the day from confidence and bravado to depression and foreboding.

The party had reserved a room at the Hotel Saskatchewan in Regina and as the polls closed at 8:00 P.M. and television coverage began, a small band of party workers and supporters had gathered to eat, drink, and offer mutual support. It was soon apparent it would be needed. John Embury had predicted NDP thirty-eight; PC fifteen; Liberals eight. The prediction had been wildly optimistic. Within half an hour of the poll's closing, an NDP landslide was being predicted, the PCs had made substantial gains, and the Liberals had been decimated. By 9:00 P.M., just two Liberals appeared even to have a chance — Roy Nelson in Assiniboia-Gravelbourg and Sonny Anderson in Shaunavon. Soon, even that hope disappeared as both slipped into second place.

The final result even was worse than most had feared. The NDP won forty-four seats and close to 48 percent of the vote; the PCs won seventeen seats and close to 38 percent of the vote; Liberals were wiped out with less than 14 percent of the vote. Ted Malone lost in his own seat to NDP candidate Doug McArthur, an impressive Rhodes scholar and former deputy minister who had taken advantage of the NDP swing and the fact that Regina Lakeview had changed substantially from the bastion of the upper class it had once been. Civil servants and working-class areas now made up the majority of the riding, and Malone saw a 777-vote plurality in 1975 change into a 982-vote deficit. Across the province, Liberals came second in three ridings (Assiniboia-Gravelbourg, Regina Lakeview, and Shaunavon) and third in fifty-eight. They attracted just 70,000 votes and more than fifty Liberal candidates lost their deposits for not receiving at least half the vote total of the winner. The new Election Act amendments on election spending and government rebates also came back to haunt the party. By attracting less than 15 percent of the vote, the party was not eligible under the law for a $75,000 government rebate.

As results poured in election night, these implications were not all immediately clear, but the overwhelming defeat could not be misinterpreted. At 9:30 P.M., a grim-faced Malone arrived at the hotel gathering. The knot of more than 100 survivors gamely applauded as he pledged: "It's not the end of the Liberal Party. It is obviously a formidable setback . . . I say we're going to come back in Saskatchewan." He said he would stay on as Liberal leader for a while "to clear up the election wreckage" but he said he would be stepping down. "Obviously, I will not be leading you for too much longer," he said. Some members of the crowd protested. Later, he told reporters he did not think the party would want him to stay on. "There's not much to lead at this point in time." His own personal future was also in doubt, since he had lost his own seat and during the previous five years of politicking, his law practice had disappeared. "Tomorrow, I look for work," he said.

It was a depressed, reserved scene at the hotel that night as shocked, numb, and sometimes incoherent survivors wandered around, crying, offering instant analysis, or simply looking for a sympathetic ear. Some were bitter and others were resigned. There were small shows of defiance and optimism. "Now, we find out who are real Liberals and who were along for the ride," Donna Welke said to no one in particular.

Malone mingled through the crowd, offering encouragement, accepting responsibility for the defeat, and offering the other parties full marks for their advances. Within a few hours, the room was empty, except for the litter left behind.

In the days ahead, the defeat and campaign would be analyzed, the future prospects considered, election-night words either reinforced or regretted.

Whatever the conclusions from those discussions, there seemed little doubt in that roomful of losers about the major message of the election. For at least a few years, the Liberal party of Saskatchewan would cease to be a major force in provincial politics. In seven years, the party had slipped from power to irrelevance.

The morning after the election, Premier Allan Blakeney held a news conference to offer his views about the success of his party's campaign. He had been the big winner, since much of the NDP effort had been centred on Blakeney's leadership. The party had been able to cash in on that, the voter uncertainty about Collver, and the Ottawa-bashing which had dominated the last few days of NDP campaigning. Blakeney told reporters his new government would fight for constitutional changes to guarantee provincial control of resources and would use the expected resource wealth to turn Saskatchewan into a "have" province, rich in assets, while retaining the pioneering spirit of the early days.

But what, asked a reporter, would be the fate of the Liberal party? Blakeney said the previous day's result might force him to change his opinion that the Liberals had a bedrock support in the province which would always keep it viable. He suggested the party had been caught in the squeeze as Saskatchewan voters polarized into a two-party system based on left-right lines. "When you get that polarization, it is very difficult for a party which gets below the 10 percent or 15 percent level to come back," he said.

Blakeney's opinions were among the multitude which surfaced in the days following the disaster. It seemed everyone had an explanation for the defeat. The *Regina Leader-Post* said the result was inevitable and implied there was little Malone could have done to stop it. Embury suggested it was in part the result of an anti-federal Liberal feeling in the province and partly that the Liberals had been caught in a crossfire between the PCs and the NDP. Voters who wanted to defeat the NDP decided the PCs were the only party capable of winning and voted Tory. Voters who wanted to keep the PCs out of office decided the NDP was the only party capable of doing that and voted NDP. Liberal Senator Sid Buckwold of Saskatoon attributed the loss to the polarization of voters and suggested the outlook for a middle-of-the-road party was bleak. "The Liberals felt they had a role to play as a middle alternative, supporting the free enterprise system yet recognizing there are social needs that require real attention," he said. "But politics in western Canada are polarizing. We're seeing the middle of the road party being squeezed out. People are either for a free enterprise group or the semi-socialist group."

There are reasons for supporting that view. The recent history of declining Liberal fortunes across western Canada is dramatic. In British Columbia and Manitoba, Liberalism has ceased to be an important provincial force as politics has divided between a left-leaning New Democratic Party and a right-leaning free enterprise party (Conservative in Manitoba and Social Credit in B.C.). In both provinces, the last Liberal MLA left the Legislature during the late seventies, although the party and its ideology of holding to the inoffensive middle ground had ceased to be attractive long before the symbolic final act was taken. The left and right parties have become so broadly based (and so non-ideological) that both take up a portion of the middle ground the Liberal party needs to survive. Alberta, so dominated by one-party politics, is a different case, but there too Liberals have disappeared from the Legislature in the face of conservative but broadly based Social Credit and Conservative parties which have straddled the ideological middle. The last Liberal MLA, William Dickie, joined the surging Conservative cause several years after his 1967 election.

Saskatchewan was the last holdout from the trend, but it was in many ways a unique situation. The brand of Liberalism practiced in Saskatchewan during the last heyday of the party was not the traditional form of Canadian liberalism. It was a right-wing brand of populism which managed to invade the traditional Conservative constituency with a combination of good organization, positive policies, and antisocialist rhetoric which deprived the Conservative party of support and kept it ineffectual and off-balance provincially. That balance began to change in the seventies when Liberals began to blur their image in search of some new voters and the Conservatives came alive with a new leader who knew how to organize and could present a vague but powerful alternative to the Liberals on the right. Liberals were caught in a crossfire and, in an increasingly desperate attempt to fight back, managed to blur their policy image even further.

However, there are other causes for the Liberal collapse to consider as well. Private New Democratic Party and Liberal polls showed the most pressing issue in the minds of most voters was the reputation of Conservative leader Collver. Allegations of underhanded business dealings (never publicly proved) and the potential for a conflict of interest if he became premier while a lawsuit against him by SGIO was still pending made most voters wary of him and anxious to make sure he did not become premier. Constituency polling completed for former Liberal MLA Merchant in September 1978 consistently shows a majority of respondents voicing negative opinions of Collver. Contrast that with the respect voiced for NDP leader Blakeney, along with the party's blatant effort to make his leadership and honesty the issue, and the outcome was inevitable. Malone was not seen as a credible alternative to Collver.

The shambles of Liberal policy also had a major effect on voter attitudes. Polls taken at the beginning of the campaign showed widespread apathy toward the Liberals, who were not seriously offering alternative policies at the time. The twenty-eight-day campaign did not substantially change the trend, although the Liberal party did lose several percentage points in the final count. In Merchant's polls, the economy was consistently the issue most often cited by voters as the most significant. In contrast to the NDP promise of prosperity through proven good management and increased resource revenues, the Liberals offered a muddle of policies which included promises of both a crackdown on unions and a cutback in government spending without any concrete proposals on how that would improve the economy and provide jobs. The Conservatives offered an untried proposal to give to the private sector Crown corporations involved in resource development, but along with other economic planks, it appeared more related to the real concerns of the voters. Interestingly, Merchant's polls also showed little voter interest in the resources issue, although the NDP campaigned heavily on resource control and credit some of their victory to that issue.

Finally, there was the shambles of Liberal organization. Despite its haste, the party managed to attract a slate of credible candidates who could have drawn some personal support despite the ineffectiveness of the general party effort. But in the final rush for the polls, organization wins elections, and across the province the Liberal party was without effective organization. Organization in the provincial office was in the hands of well-meaning amateurs, and at the local level it often simply did not exist. Polls were often not canvassed, the vote was not identified, and workers acted without effective leadership and without direction. Ironically, the Conservatives also suffered some organizational problems, despite their reputation for organization. In many urban constituencies considered potential wins, Tory canvassing was sporadic and voter identification inadequate. The NDP machine was effective in most areas, although the final results showed the NDP to be an increasingly urban party. It swept all the seats in Saskatoon, Prince Albert, and Moose Jaw and lost just one in Regina, while losing several rural areas. The Conservatives lost both urban seats won in the 1977 by-elections, but won sixteen of their seventeen seats in largely rural areas where their organization and policy appeal were greater. Agricultural and rural policy, once the cutting edge of NDP innovations, had ceased to excite many rural voters. The urban middle class was increasingly claiming the NDP as its own.

Throughout the fall of 1978, Liberal leaders held meetings to consider the implications of their defeat and the tasks which lay ahead. The immediate challenges were clear. In late October, Malone agreed to remain as leader and that made the most pressing problem financial. The party emerged from the election close to $200,000 in debt, and the question was whether or not money could be raised to meet the obligations and pay Malone a salary without selling the Regina headquarters purchased six years earlier when there was money to spare. It soon became clear there would be no financial help from the provincial government. Saskatchewan election law allows for a rebate to parties of $75,000 if they receive at least 15 percent of the vote in an election. Liberal votes represented just 13.9 percent of the total and, despite pleas from Malone for an exception, the government would not agree and no rebate was paid. Many constituencies also fell short of the 15 percent needed to qualify for a rebate on local spending.

When the party met for its annual convention in March 1979, Treasurer Ian McLellan recommended the headquarters be sold. However, fund-raising returns for 1978 showed federal and provincial income for the year totalled $268,522, plus a $100,000 loan from the Bank of Nova Scotia. It included close to $200,000 raised by local Liberal organizations, $23,000 in memberships, and $36,000 from corporations. During the winter, Malone also became a more effective fund-raiser and by spring, he announced the headquarters would not have to be sold and by using it as security to consolidate debts, they would slowly be paid off.

Although securing a better long-term financial outlook was vital, party planners also had some immediate organizational tasks facing them that winter. A federal election was just months away, and while hopes were dimming for a good showing, it was important to identify the 1978 vote as a base for future building. The 70,000 people who supported the lost cause provincially were considered a good beginning, and with former MLA Jack Wiebe elected as provincial party president and Senator Dave Steuart as provincial campaign chairman for the federal fight, two organizers were in charge.

The fight to save some or all of the three federal Liberal seats in Saskatchewan became the focus of party hopes for the future.

Chapter Fourteen

DEFEAT OF THE LANG GANG

Waiting for Prime Minister Trudeau to call the federal election was an exercise in frustration for Saskatchewan Liberal planners. With each delay, their prospects dimmed. With each passing month, the party's tenuous hold on popularity was slipping.

The slide really began during the winter of 1977-78, after several false election starts. To that point, prospects appeared to be the brightest in years and planners were confident of winning five or six seats out of the fourteen seats available. Despite provincial Liberal troubles, federal government rail rehabilitation programs and Canadian wheat board sales appeared to be making the party popular. In late 1977, Senator Steuart was appointed provincial campaign chairman, and with the three sitting MPs apparently safe, Tony Merchant and Stuart Cameron running in Regina, and several other high-profile candidates prepared to stand, he was buoyant. "I could have guaranteed five seats then, probably more," he said later. In 1978, the optimism began to dim as poll results and field reports began to indicate an anti-Trudeau, antigovernment feeling was spreading. In the face of this and the obvious collapse of the provincial organization, Steuart revised his prediction down to three MPs.

By the winter of 1979, private polls commissioned by the party showed Liberals trailing in all but Tony Merchant's Regina East seat. Even Transport Minister Lang was in a fight in his Saskatoon East seat with a popular priest, Bob Ogle, running for the NDP and Tory businessman Dan Meyers. In Regina, Merchant's private polls showed his spring 1978 approval rating of 70 percent had dropped to close to 40 percent, just 10 percentage points ahead of New Democrat Simon de Jong.

In March 1979, Trudeau called the election for May 22. Liberals threw themselves into the fight hoping to salvage one or two seats. In all but a couple of ridings, they campaigned on the record of the Liberal government and Otto Lang — $900 million pledged to upgrade rail lines, action taken to improve grain handling facilities, promises of more to come — and belittled the leadership and program potential of the PCs. The New Democrats centred their campaign on resource control, the need to control prices and create jobs, and the need to "save" the national medicare plan from the policies of the Liberal and Conservatives. The PCs campaigned to remove the Liberals after sixteen years of government and, along the way, they promised improved grain handling, programs for middle-class home owners, and stricter controls on public sector power.

When the ballots were counted May 22, the Liberals had been wiped out, the PCs had won ten seats, and the NDP had picked up four but found itself confined largely to urban areas. Otto Lang, after eleven years of power, ran third with 30.5 percent of the vote in Saskatoon East. Fr. Ogle claimed the seat for the NDP. Cliff McIsaac ran third behind the PCs and NDP with 25 percent of the Battlefords-Meadow Lake vote. Fifteen consecutive years in provincial and federal politics were ended for the North Battleford veterinarian. Ralph Goodale lost his Assiniboia seat to a Conservative and ran third with 29 percent of the vote. Tony Merchant, after two years of campaigning and expenditures of more than $100,000, ran third with 30.6 percent of the vote in Regina East. Stuart Cameron lost to the NDP and ran third with 26 percent of the vote in Regina West.

Across the province, the party was battered. It received just 21.7 percent of the votes cast — 106,000 of 490,000. Eight of fourteen Liberal candidates lost their deposits after receiving less than half the vote total of the winner. Although money had not been a campaign problem, the party came out of the election $100,000 in debt, adding to the provincial debt from the previous fall.

Nationally, sixteen years of Liberal government ended when PC leader Joe Clark won a minority mandate. Provincially, the party reached its lowest point in more than a decade (throughout most of the sixties, no Liberal MPs were elected in Saskatchewan).

In the aftermath of the election, Liberals were quick to attribute the loss to the national anti-Trudeau mood and voter desire to change governments after sixteen years. There is no doubt that is partially valid, but there are other, more complex reasons as well. Policy, personalities, and organizational failures all played a part.

In Saskatchewan, as elsewhere, the Liberals offered few policy alternatives during the campaign. National promises of strong leadership, an aggressive energy policy, and control on government spending were uninspiring and often hollow offers from a government which had frequently seemed to act in direct opposition to these ideas during the previous eleven years. There were no overall Saskatchewan policy proposals or attractive alternatives. On the negative side were countless small blocs of voters alienated by specific Liberal or Lang policies — antiabortionists who felt the Liberals were disregarding life by allowing therapeutic abortions (although Lang was a strong antiabortion Catholic); anti-French Anglos who felt Quebec and French Canadians had too much power in the Liberal government; voters who objected to the switch to metric measure, considering it more French influence; voters who objected to Lang's anti-capital-punishment stand and the abolition of capital punishment during the Trudeau years. "These might be small blocks of 500 or 600 people, but taken together, they were important," said Lang's campaign manager Tom Molloy.

The public image of an arrogant government, along with public dissatisfaction about some of Lang's foibles in the previous five years, also came back to haunt the party. Lang had received extensive coverage from an often hostile media about use of government jets to fly around the country, use of government transport to bring a nanny for his seven children from Great Britain to Ottawa, and total refusal to concede any ground to political opponents. His response to critics was usually either a spirited defense of himself or a simple refusal to admit he was wrong. Public humility was not one of his strong points. To many critics, he exemplified the image of government aloofness and crass political superiority. In Regina, brother-in-law Merchant did not help his own cause by an abundance of excesses — flaunting the spirit of election spending restraints by lavishing money on advertising, brochures, and a flower for most voters on election day; distributing federal government grants during the election campaign although he had no right to do so; and issuing campaign literature which implied he was both the incumbent MP and had experience in government — both untrue.

There were also errors in organization, although it is doubtful that a flawless organizational campaign would have made much difference. The problems centred on the federal-provincial split which had been developing for a decade. In 1977 when Steuart was named campaign chairman by Trudeau, with the support of Lang, he assumed the title meant he would be in charge, with the staff, resources, and support to do the job. However, he quickly found he was to have a minor role in a very fragmented campaign. Lang, Merchant, Cameron, Goodale, and McIsaac all had separate campaign organizations operating under the guidance of the federal affairs committee. Steuart said later he found himself working with the demoralized provincial Liberal organization, trying simply to put up a pretense of a fight in the nine ridings in which the Liberal candidate had little chance. "When I was made chairman, my clear feeling was that the prime minister wanted me to take over," he said later. "I thought that as the election drew closer, the campaign committee would take over from the federal affairs committee to run the operation. But I soon found out these little pockets of power had no intention of giving any of it up. They really wanted me as a figurehead to coordinate and look after the balance of the seats."

Meanwhile, in Saskatoon at the federal affairs committee and in the Lang organization, there was growing dissatisfaction with Steuart and the role he was playing. Molloy said they felt Steuart was not providing leadership for the provincial campaign and the separate organizations continued for want of such leadership. "I guess we were disappointed at the extent of his effect," said Molloy.

It was the final, logical split between the provincial and federal forces, extended into the federal campaign. The result was that the Saskatchewan campaign lacked coherence. The team effect, led by Lang in 1974 and coordinated to concentrate resources and staff in key, winnable ridings, did not develop. "We ended up with 14 different campaigns and I didn't really have a very important function," said Steuart.

Better coordination would likely have meant little to the May 22, 1979, election rout the Liberals suffered. Its major effect would have been to make the job a little easier when post-election Liberal survivors gathered to try to patch together a future for the party in Saskatchewan.

AFTERMATH OF DEFEAT

Within a week of the election disaster, the federal-provincial battle for control of the Saskatchewan party was on again. As before, the battleground was money. Provincial officials were insisting they should have a say over distribution and control of money collected through the federal tax rebate program. Federal affairs committee officials wanted to have the same power. After some heated meetings, a committee was established to consider the issue of controlling the money, with the power to make recommendations to both the provincial executive and the federal affairs committee. Ted Malone and Jack Wiebe represented the Saskatchewan Liberal Association on the committee. Otto Lang and Tom Molloy represented the federal affairs committee. With a fifth member to be appointed by Trudeau, it would be the major arena for feuding in the months ahead.

With more than $200,000 in debts and a federal election likely within two years, the emphasis had to be on raising money and reconstructing an election machine. However, with most party leaders conceding themselves at least a few years in the wilderness, it was also important that the party examine some fundamental questions about its flaws and its future. The example of the Liberals in 1959 and the Progressive Conservatives in 1973 offered proof that predictions of the death of the party need not come true. But some basic questions of leadership, organization, and policy would have to be resolved if the party was to avoid becoming the fringe group it has been reduced to elsewhere in the West. The answer to the party collapse lay partly in the circumstances and issues of the day, but also partly within the provincial party itself and the mistakes it made during and after its days of power.

If history teaches Saskatchewan Liberals anything, it is that the root of political success is organization. Ross Thatcher and Dave Steuart knew that in the early sixties and built an organization which delivered. Then, they failed to keep it active and alive with new blood and new ideas. As the leader pulled more power into his own office, the organization became less an integral part of the Liberal political process and more simply a machine to win an election every four years.

Steuart inherited this decaying machine and, despite elaborate plans and money spent, he was unable to reverse the trend and to put his own stamp on the party. It was too top heavy, waiting to be directed from Regina. The middle-level, local workers required to keep the organization alive were not performing their function and were not successfully motivated to do it. Malone's inept approach and almost total lack of preparation for the election added the final, dramatic push to the process.

A new provincial Liberal party would have to begin to build at the constituency level and forget the idea that it can be directed and defined from Regina. It would have to learn again the basics of fund raising, membership sales, and grass-roots politicking.

There is also a lesson in the history books about policy. Liberals like to consider themselves "middle of the road" and argue this will appeal to those voters uncomfortable with ideological extremes. Steuart argues the party must be careful not to "change too much" in its philosophical approach. The reality, however, is that the Saskatchewan party has little clearly-defined philosophy. In the past decade, it has responded to the whim of public opinion, hoping to benefit from whatever the current trend was. In 1975, it opposed growing government while offering programs which would contribute to that growth. In 1978, Liberal planners grasped at what they felt was a public mood of disenchantment with Big Labor, Big Government and Big Politics. In neither election did the platform ring true as a reflection of a well-defined political philosophy. Power, or hating the left, is no longer an adequate sustaining philosophy. While many Liberals said the party looked inward after 1975 to find what liberalism meant, the result still seemed to many to be expediency and shallowness which failed either to inspire party workers or to convert voters. The party has appeared to be an organization with few common themes and little higher purpose.

Since Ross Thatcher's vision of tough government and an industrial Saskatchewan was repudiated, the Liberal party has been drifting. If the political culture has undergone a polarization, the challenge for the Liberals is to stake out some territory, develop an intellectual and policy framework flexible enough to be adapted to day-to-day situations, and then stick to it. It would be a gamble that voters will eventually start to come back, but the alternative of straying over the political map in search of votes leaves a party with little to offer on the philosophical firing line but a taste for power.

The issue of leadership must also be confronted. After the 1978 election defeat, many in the party felt Thatcher, Steuart, and Malone had let them down, each in their own way. Thatcher was too unbending, authoritarian, and strong-willed to let the party have a soul and a life of its own. Steuart led it on a search for new strength and ideas but in the end was too weak to hammer the result into a concise and winning combination while keeping the organization renewed. Malone failed the ultimate test of keeping the party prepared for an election and strong at the constituency level.

All those arguments contain some truth but it is also true that the party let its leaders down. Liberals had become too used to strong leaders who did things for them. They were too willing to be bossed around, too anxious for power to try to disrupt the vertical power lines if it meant less efficiency in the drive for election. In the end, the party looked to Malone to fight the election battle and he had neither the experience, support, nor charisma to patch the party together for the battle.

Finally, there is the troubling issue of federal-provincial relations within the Liberal party. During almost two decades of tension between federal and provincial factions within the organization, separate structures evolved. The Lang organization gained power and influence as federal fortunes rose and he attracted the loyalties of key Liberal thinkers and organizers, as well as a source of income from federal campaign legislation. The split originated after Lang and federal Liberals felt it necessary to protect federal interests in the face of hostile provincial Liberals. Its growth was almost always at the expense of the provincial organization. Constitutionally the provincial party is supreme and it has traditionally been the main party fund-raiser and controller of the money. But as its power began to ebb to the federal wing, provincial leaders tried to find some accommodation. Rather than insisting on maintaining primacy, with a split in the pary as the ultimate bargaining point, Steuart, and then Malone, acquiesced. A separate federal group was formally established and recognized, and then federal election-law changes gave the federal wing control over much of the money. Soon the powerful Lang seemed to set the tone for all Liberals in the province. Provincial party members were often in the position of defending unpopular federal positions and in the end, the party was reduced to the position of hoping for federal strength so it could ride on Lang's coattails.

The reality of politics is that the interests and policies of federal and provincial Liberal leaders will often be at odds. The question facing the party is whether that means two separate organizations, usually with the same workers, should evolve to make the difference clear to voters? If not, which wing should dominate the organization and determine the priorities? Molloy said shortly after the election it is important that the federal affairs committee be retained and that a federal leader and spokesman be maintained in the province to represent federal Liberal interests. Steuart took a different view. "There is one party, one provincial leader, Ted Malone, and one president, Jack Wiebe, and that is how it should be," he said. "We face the same situation now we did in 1959. We had been dominated from Ottawa by Jimmy Gardiner and it hurt us. In 1958, he was beaten and we blossomed. Now, we can blossom again."

The 1980s began with the questions still unanswered. In fact, instead of the quiet renewal many Liberals were hoping would begin, the new decade began with yet another humiliating defeat for the party in Saskatchewan. The federal Progressive Conservative minority government of Prime Minister Joe Clark survived just seven months before being defeated in a parliamentary non-confidence vote in December 1979. On February 18, 1980, after a two-month winter election campaign remembered more for its Clark jokes and Liberal vagueness than for serious debate of issues, the voters returned Pierre Trudeau and the Liberal party to a majority government. Final Commons standings were: Liberals 147; PCs 103; NDP 32. The Conservatives lost heavily to the Liberals in Atlantic and central Canada and to the NDP in the West. The New Democrats won the most seats in the party's history by winning big in Manitoba, Saskatchewan, and British Columbia while losing seats in Newfoundland, Nova Scotia, and Ontario. The Liberals scored major gains in the Atlantic provinces and Ontario, while sweeping seventy-four of seventy-five seats in Quebec (the biggest Liberal sweep in that province since 1921). However, in the West, the governing party was stymied. Two Liberals were re-elected in Manitoba, but west of Winnipeg, the party came up empty-handed.

Increasingly, Canada was becoming a nation of regional parties, jockeying for power without any clear cause for claiming national support or national vision. With no recent tradition of coalition governments and no political leaders of the power-broker stature of Sir John A. Macdonald or William Lyon Mackenzie King to arbitrate between conflicting interests when formulating national policy, the outcome of the February 18 election was a grim sign post. National governments, almost by definition it seemed, were becoming divisive — the representative of one region and the perceived oppressor of another. Within days of the result, worried westerners looked at the Ontario and Quebec-centred government and began to talk seriously of western separatism. While Liberal leaders promised to find some way to include westerners in the decision-making, the nation was clearly uneasy as the 1980s began.

In Saskatchewan, the major election trend was a swing to the New Democratic Party. The NDP gained two seats from the Conservatives and the two parties split the fourteen seats evenly. For Liberals, the vote was largely a disaster — the third straight election in which the party had failed to elect a single federal or provincial member. Former MPs Ralph Goodale and Dr. Cliff McIsaac tried and failed to regain their Commons seats. High-spending Tony Merchant ran again in Regina and collected a lower percentage of the popular vote than he had nine months previously — 28 percent compared to 30.6 percent. In Saskatoon East, the former stronghold of Otto Lang, newcomer candidate Doug Richardson ran a strong campaign but still placed third with the same 30.5 percent of the vote Lang collected in his 1979 defeat. Although still somewhat involved in the Saskatchewan party, Lang played no obvious election role. Shortly after May 1979, he was named a vice-president of Pioneer Grain Company of Winnipeg and the move to Winnipeg made him less a factor in the province.

For the truly dedicated, February 18, 1980, did contain some bright spots for Saskatchewan Liberals. The party's share of the popular vote climbed from 21.7 percent to 24.2 percent and Liberal candidates attracted over 107,000 votes. Two Liberals ran second, compared to uniform third place showings in 1979. And in one obvious piece of good news, the party showed some startling life in Prince Albert — once a Liberal stronghold which sent Sir Wilfrid Laurier and William Lyon Mackenzie King to Ottawa as prime ministers[1] but a wasteland since 1953 when John Diefenbaker won it and then held it until his death in August 1979. In a November 1979 by-election, the seat went to New Democrat Stan Hovdebo by 600 votes over the PCs. Liberal candidate Clyne Harradence, a well-known, aggressive, and quick-tongued local lawyer, ran a distant third. On February 18, Harradence picked up more than 3,000 votes and came within 800 votes of unseating Hovdebo. The showing gave Liberals the hope that Prince Albert may be within their grasp again.

The campaign also offered some prospect that the level of federal-provincial feuding in the party may be declining. Provincial president Jack Wiebe and federal affairs committee representative Tom Molloy were co-chairmen of the campaign and the tensions of recent campaigns were not visible. A series of high-profile federal Liberals, including Pierre Trudeau, campaigned in the province and from the provincial side, Wiebe and leader Ted Malone were both active.

Still, despite the few good signs, the campaign was largely a bad Liberal experience. The party was confirmed once again in the unfamiliar role as a Saskatchewan also-ran. The easy election-night explanation from a number of provincial spokesmen was that the anti-Trudeau mood of May 1979 was still visible and damaging enough to lose Liberal seats in the West. The image of the leader was clearly an issue and in many cases a negative one for Liberals, but reasons for the poor showing were more varied and complex than simply the presence of Trudeau.

The campaign platform for the West was largely uninspiring. Nationally, opinion polls showed the major issues were leadership, the brief record of the Clark government (with a disastrous series of policy reversals or errors to its credit), and a Tory budget which promised tough government action to control spending and substantially higher fossil fuel costs through both higher well-head prices for petroleum and an eighteen-cent-per-gallon excise tax on gasoline. On the Prairies, those concerns were supplemented by worry over high interest rates and government efforts to improve the grain handling system.

---

[1] Laurier never actually served as Prince Albert MP. In 1896, he was elected in both Prince Albert, then called Saskatchewan riding, and Quebec East. When he was named prime minister after the election and became part of the cabinet, the law of the day required that he resign and seek personal re-election. He chose to run in Quebec East and a new MP was elected in Prince Albert. King represented the constituency from 1926 until his defeat in 1945.

While Liberals elsewhere were largely content to offer vague policy promises in the knowledge that simply by being an alternative to the unpopular Clark, they were picking up support, on the Prairies they offered some specific plums to try to win back lost ground. Party campaign material assured westerners that they too were "founding peoples" with an important role to play in the future of the country and the national unity debate. "Western Liberals are determined, working within a national political party with a proud Canadian history and within a national Liberal government, to ensure fairness and realistic support for western agriculture, transportation, energy, secondary industry . . . in short, the people of western Canada," party election campaign material promised. As with much of the rest of Liberal campaigning, there were few specifics on which to judge the promises, but there were some — eliminate fuel taxes proposed in the Conservative budget; allow salaries paid to farm spouses to be deducted for income tax purposes; increase money available for agricultural research; give farmers a break on the amount of capital gains they must pay when selling their farms; develop a new National Transportation Act guaranteeing statutory freight rates on grain movement; and double-track the CNR main line from Winnipeg to Vancouver to increase hauling capacity.

Voter response to the promise to eliminate the threatened fuel tax was generally positive. Reaction to the double-tracking proposal, a very expensive proposition of dubious need, was generally skeptical. Otherwise, there was little reaction to the platform or to the fact that it said nothing about high interest rates, a major farm issue in light of massive farm debt throughout the Prairies. Perhaps voters were more interested in a policy question not addressed by the Liberals: Could Pierre Trudeau be trusted to understand the West any better now than he had done in his previous terms as prime minister? Were Liberal promises of a new interest in the West sincere and practical, or were they simply the political rantings of a man and a party hungry for votes and power? Whatever answer individual voters arrived at, three out of four in Saskatchewan decided not to vote Liberal.

Organization was also a problem area for the party. Both the New Democrats and the Progressive Conservatives could look for support and constituency work from strong provincial machines. The Liberals did not have that luxury. Since the election debacle in October 1978, little had been done to rebuild the provincial party. Malone had been kept on as leader, but he was functioning only part-time while trying to re-establish his Regina law practice. Jack Wiebe was proving to be an active president and efforts by party leaders to reduce the debt inherited from the 1978 and 1979 campaigns had been having some effect. However, nothing resembling an effective party organization had been created across the province. Except for occasional statements from leaders on current events or organizational plans no significant effort had been made to redefine the party, develop an intellectual and policy framework, or reverse the negative image of the party held by the public. Even the delicate issue of federal-provincial

Liberal relations remained uncertain, although it was far less explosive than during the days when Otto Lang was a more active force in provincial politics.

During the summer of 1979, a University of Saskatchewan professor and sometime Liberal candidate, C.M. Williams, was appointed the fifth member of the committee established to work out financial arrangements between the two wings. The work of the committee was low-key and the tension of the issue had clearly dissipated somewhat since there was no obvious power base in either wing of the party and no immediate prize to be won. By late April 1980, Williams was predicting a compromise position would evolve from the committee by the summer, offering provincial Liberals more control over the funds collected through the federal tax-rebate program and in other fund-collecting drives. Williams said he expected all money raised to be split evenly between the two wings of the party, with the committee overseeing the fund comprised of both federal and provincial representatives. When a compromise was reached, it would have to be submitted to federal and provincial Liberal leaders for ratification.

One uncertainty added to the situation was the March 1980 appointment of Senator Hazen Argue as the Saskatchewan representative in the federal cabinet. He was appointed by Prime Minister Trudeau because there were no elected Liberals in Saskatchewan and one of the areas of Argue's mandate was to provide a link between federal and provincial Liberals during the rebuilding period. It was a strange choice by Trudeau. Argue, as a former CCF leader and one-time bitter enemy of Ross Thatcher, was not well liked by Saskatchewan Liberals and he had not played a significant role in party affairs since switching to the party in 1962 after losing the battle with T.C. Douglas to become the first leader of the national New Democratic Party. Argue's appointment held the potential for further federal-provincial conflict, since Saskatchewan Liberals would likely resent overt moves by the left-leaning senator to give them directions.

Still, there was a spirit of compromise in evidence. Many Liberals realized if the party was ever to mount a serious threat again or to provide an organizational base for future federal or provincial campaigns, the structural flaws would have to be corrected. And if those efforts bear fruit with increased electoral support, the federal-provincial antagonisms will have to be settled or the problems of the 1970s could easily surface again.

The history of politics in Saskatchewan is the story of a two-party system. The United Farmers of Canada had strength but did not create a dynasty as it did in Alberta. Its energies were absorbed by the then-powerful Liberal party. The Conservatives and Progressives combined in 1929 to throw the Liberals out, but soon disappeared themselves. The Social Credit party rose and disappeared within a few years. Throughout that history, the Liberal party was the constant thread, linking the province's expectant, founding days to its halcyon, affluent, smug mood of the late seventies.

Now, continuation of that assured spot at the centre of political affairs in the province is in doubt. In the wake of three disastrous elections, Liberal leaders are left with 100,000 voters who could be a foundation on which to build a future. The challenge facing party leaders is to recreate an organization, to fashion a credible creed, and to develop the leadership capable of articulating party strengths and pointing out the foibles of their political opponents. That done, it will be left to time and the voters to determine if Liberalism has become the latest victim of Saskatchewan's two-party nature.

INDEX

Agriculture
  1975 Liberal policy on, 66
  Liberal attack on NDP policy, 75
Blakeney, Allan
  elected Saskatchewan
    premier, 25
  history of, 25
  popularity of, 88
  doubtful of Liberal
    comeback, 151
By-elections
  Athabasca, 47
  Prince Albert, 123
  Saskatoon Sutherland, 123
Caucus, Liberal
  after 1971 election, 25
  opposition to NDP, 26
  assessment of 1971-75
    caucus, 72-73
  Legislature performance, 74-77
Collver, Dick
  elected Conservative leader, 83
  rebuilds PC party, 84
  under public attack, 135
  liability to party, 152
Development, forestry
  Prince Albert pulp mill
    opened, 18-19
  Athabasca plant proposed, 20
  Athabasca deal cancelled, 26

Development, mining
  Thatcher attitude towards, 12
  potash industry declines, 19
  1975 Liberal policy on, 66
Elections
  1960, Liberals gain, 10
  1964, Liberals win, 12
  1967, Thatcher re-elected, 16
  1971, NDP elected, 22
  1975, NDP re-elected, 94
  1978, Liberals wiped out, 149
Election, 1975
  campaign begins, 87
  party platforms, 88-89
  campaign tactics, 90-91
  Liberal organization
    flawed, 91-93
Election, 1978
  campaign begins, 139
  party platforms, 141-146
  Liberal organization: unprepared,
    137; search for candidates, 140-
    141
  Liberal policy: written by com-
    mittee, 141-143; unpopular,
    143-144
  Liberal strategy: nominations de-
    layed, 134; tactic backfires, 137;
    campaign plan, 144-146; attack
    on Collver, 148

Election, 1979 federal Liberals
early confidence, 155
total defeat, 156
campaign problems, 156-157
Election, 1980
all Liberals defeated, 162
Liberal campaign policy, 163-164
organization lacking, 164
Embury, John
elected party president, 103
feuds with Lang, 127

Federal-provincial feud, Liberal
1960, Thatcher versus Lang, 13
Steuart conciliatory, 32, 51
history of dispute, 51-52
role of Otto Lang, 53-54
federal-provincial split, 54-55
federal fund-raising
dominance, 56-57
effect on 1975 election, 95
factor in race for president, 102
factor in leadership race, 113, 116
1977 dispute over funds, 127
effect on 1979 campaign
loss, 157
Finances, Liberal party
Thatcher's legacy, 27
Steuart fund raising, 46
effect of Election Expenses
Act, 55
coffers full, 82, 89
federals and provinces feud, 127
provincial coffers empty, 130
party in debt, 153
deficit increases, 156
Fraser, Gerry
policy committee chairman, 61
criticism of leadership, 69
declines to run for leader, 114
by-election candidate, 122
Freight rates
Crowsnest pass freight rates, 80
Lang suggests changes, 81

Saskatchewan Liberals hurt by
issue, 82
Ideology, Liberal party
antisocialism, 60
1975 confusion, 65
Labor
Thatcher attitude toward, 16
Steuart distrust of unions, 39
campaign attacks, 90
1978 Liberal policy on, 147
Land Bank, 22, 74
Lane, Gary
leadership prospect, 100
conflict with Steuart, 101, 102
leadership candidate, 112
withdraws from race, 113
joins Tories, 118
Lang, Otto
1960 feud with Thatcher, 13
federal campaign chairman, 13, 53
leader of Thatcher
opposition, 53
description, 53
elected to Parliament, 54
leads 'fed' organization, 53-55
an issue in presidential
election, 103
defeated as MP, 156
as issue in 1979 campaign, 157
takes grain industry job, 162
Leader Post, Regina
supports Liberal, 75, 78
predicts Liberal demise, 148
Leadership, Thatcher
style of, 13
autocratic, 20
offers to resign, 24
Leadership race, 1971, 27-31
Leadership race, 1976, 112
federal influence, 116
campaign bitterness, 117
Malone wins, 119
Leith, George, 29
effect on 1971 leadership, 30
influence through 171 Club, 63

Liberal Party, Saskatchewan
  1950s decline, 7
  gains under Thatcher, 10, 12
  dominated by Thatcher, 20, 45
  defeated by NDP, 22
  loses leader, 24
  organizational flaws, 43
  decentralization, 45, 47
  Steuart successes, 47
  decline and demoralized, 121,
    126, 127
  by-election losses, 123, 125
  loses 'Official Opposition'
    status, 130
  Legislature seats lost, 149
  federal seats lost, 156
  assessing future, 159
Liberally, 100, 101
Liberals, federal
  role in provincial convention, 31
  Lang leadership, 53-54
  separate Saskatchewan organiza-
    tion, 54
  controlling funds, 57
MacDonald, Cy, 27, 29
Malone, Ted
  elected to Legislature, 47
  leadership candidate, 112
  history, 114
  leadership race tactics, 115
  campaign policies, 116-117
  wins leadership, 119
  as leader: initial challenges, 122;
    loses by-elections, 123, 125; un-
    able to stop decline, 128-129;
    outlines policy, 129; failure to
    motivate, 132-133; election
    strategy, 134; effective cam-
    paigner, 144; loses seat, 149;
    remains leader, 153
McDonald, A. H., 7
  deposed as leader, 8
  attempt at policy reform, 59
Media, Liberals critical of, 92, 148
Medicare
  Liberal attitude toward, 10-11, 15

issue in 1979 campaign, 156
Merchant, Tony, 100
  leadership candidate, 112
  history, 114
  leadership campaign tactics, 115
  defeated, 119
  critical of Malone, 123
  unsuccessful federal candidate,
    156, 162
New Democratic Party
  elected to power, 22
  initiatives in government, 74
  attitudes to business, 74
  re-elected, 94
  gears for 1978 election, 136, 139
  fears Liberal collapse, 139
  1978 election platform, 145
  re-elected, 149
Oil industry, taxation
  NDP policy, 76
  Liberal criticism, 76
  federal-provincial dispute, 80
  tax illegal; Liberals confused, 130,
    131
171 Club, 63
Organization, Liberal party
  after 1971 defeat, 27
  reorganization plan, 44
  1972-75 successes, flaws, 47-49
  decline under Malone, 121, 127-
    129
Policy, Liberal party
  historic outlook, 60, 61
  Steuart reform plan, 59
  policy committees, 62-64
  1975 platform, 65-67
  see also election, 1978
Potash industry
  Saskatchewan history, 104-105
  NDP policy toward, 105
  Liberal policy toward, 106
  government takeover, 106-108
  1978 election issue, 147
Progressive Conservatives
  Liberal perspective, 14, 84
  Saskatchewan history, 83

resurgence, 84–85
1975 gains, 92–94
issue in Liberal leadership race, 118–119
by-election wins, 123
momentum slows, 135
1978 election platform, 145
election gains, 149
Referenda, Liberal proposal for, 143–144
Senate
  Steuart lobbies for appointment, 99
  Steuart appointed to, 111
Star-Phoenix, Saskatoon, 95
Steuart, Dave
  history: influence of father, 34; introduction to unions, 34; political start, 35; elected to Prince Albert council, 36; becomes MLA, 37; appointed senator, 111; 1979 Saskatchewan campaign manager, 157
  as leader: elected 29–31; approach to caucus, 71; performance in Legislature, 73–77; antisocialist rhetoric, 74–75; trips out of province, 77–79; relations with federal Liberals, 79–80; Crow rate controversy, 81; leadership weakness, 49, 62, 68; announces retirement, 99; criticized by caucus, 101; considers resigning, 102
  with Ross Thatcher: challenges A. H. McDonald, 8; Thatcher

booster, 9; organizer, 10; wins by-election, 11; health minister, 15; finance minister, 17; deputy premier, 37; party mediator, 38
  philosophy: free enterprise advocate, 34, 38; distrust of unions, 39; anti-bureaucrat, 39; social conscience, 64; conclusions about Liberals, 68; Cold War rhetoric, 74, 75
  in 1975 election: popularity, 88; attacks unions, 90; negative campaign, 91; weakness evident, 93; criticized by media, 95; self-analysis, 97
Thatcher, Colin, 94, 126
Thatcher government
  first term optimism, 14
  free enterprise attitude, 15
  wins re-election, 16
  second term pessimism, 17
  popularity loss, 19–21
Thatcher, Ross
  as alternative to A. H. McDonald, 8
  becomes Liberal leader, 9
  Mossbank debate, 10
  rebuilds party, 10
  fights with federal Liberals, 13, 14
  1967 campaign, 16, 22
  death of, 24
  dominated party, 45
Wilson, Garry, 31
Women's rights, 67, 68

Barry Wilson grew up on a small farm in Quebec. He took his post-secondary education at Carleton University in Ottawa where he was awarded a Bachelor of Arts in Political Science and an Honors Degree in Journalism.

The author has worked for a number of newspapers in eastern and western Canada. While reporting for the Saskatoon *Star-Phoenix*, he was able to view political developments in Saskatchewan first-hand.

Barry Wilson currently is the Ottawa correspondent for *The Western Producer*.